The Lege
Robin hood

Richard Rutherford-Moore

The Legend of Robin Hood

©1998 Richard Rutherford-Moore

ISBN 1 898307

ALL RIGHTS RESERVED

Cover design by Paul Mason
Front cover photo shows the author as an authentically recreated *Forester of Sherwood* AD1200; blending "folk and fairy tales, fact and natural history" guiding tour parties in Sherwood Forest based on this book
Cover photograph by Nic Broomhead of the Notts Tourist Unit

Published by:

Capall Bann Publishing
Freshfields
Chieveley
Berks
RG20 8TF

Acknowledgements to :

Mr & Mrs Lees
Nottingham City Museum & Local Studies Library
Sherwood Forest Visitor Centre & Forest Rangers
Heath Pye & The Wolfshead Bowmen
Tony & Jo of the Spirit of England Medieval Theatre Group
The Kings Clipstone local study group
The Tales of Robin Hood, Nottingham
Nottinghamshire Tourist Office
Histrionix Living History Group

And my little Wife for putting up with it all

The photographs were all taken by the author; who is available from 1998 as a guide/companion for visitors following the outlaw trail to the places mentioned in the text

e-mail *r&j@armor.demon.co.uk* **for the author**

Special thanks to the faeryfolk of the Hollow Hills and Annwn; the patience of Robin Hood himself and the Sherwood Archers for demonstrating to me the simplistic power and accuracy of the English longbow; Richard the Lionheart for his honest kingship; to Izzi, Debbie and Andy, merry-persons at the Sherwood Forest Visitor Centre; to Nottingham Local Studies Library; and to all the parish churchwardens who care for the historic old churches here in north Nottinghamshire.

On The Outlaw Trail

Writing *The Legend of Robin Hood* from late autumn last year through to early summer has has been one of the most enjoyable things I've ever done.

I've met some wonderfully friendly people, always ready to tell a story or lead you through leafy bower and over stream to seek out a beautiful but seldom visited spot, then having a refreshing cup of tea by invitation in their beautiful well-kept gardens, standing high in the Peak District looking over vistas of hill and dale; or by contrast walking in the dappled shade of the old oaks of Sherwood Forest chatting about natural history; or dabbling your toes in the River Trent on a hot day whilst your bicycle lies nearby in the long grass, watching an archer fletching his arrows and recounting tales of Robin Hood; by night under the stars, debating the origin of ancient rituals by candle or firelight in sacred space with folk who trusted me with their religious beliefs as a fellow seeker; or hearing the ffftt-putt sound of a handmade arrow thudding into the gold of a straw boss at sixty yards, shot by a skillful and traditional longbowman.

I hope the reader will want to follow the outlaw trail as I did in Sherwood Forest. Its a treat in store! Additional material for a pre-tour prep is listed at the end of the text; your local library will supply lots more.

Unfortunately, the planned size of this book does not permit me to include a full printing of the main ballads featuring

Robin Hood. However, there are three works available that do, and all very reasonably priced. I began with Jim Lee's booklet *The Legendary Exploits of Robin Hood in Nottingham* (£1.50; Temple Nostalgia Press, Nottingham).

Contents

Dedicated to the merry men and women
of our Armed and Emergency Services
and the staff in our National Health Service

Thank You for Being There

Introduction to the Author

Richard Rutherford-Moore has been a keen walker, camper and sportsman since boyhood - born and bred only a quarter mile from Loxley, one of the claimants for Robin Hood's birthplace. He fired his first antique muzzle-loading gun at a very early age, was bitten by the history bug and continued to research this aspect in a practical sense, living outdoors in primitive conditions or performing period historical survival training in researching and recreating the past.

He created a historical soldier-character of Wellington's Army, interpreting him at displays all over the United Kingdom for over twenty-five years, before serving as the Military & Technical Adviser on the highly successful *Sharpe* television series 1992-7, based on Bernard Cornwell's best-selling novels. Richard worked on both sides of the camera; adding the period military tactics and drill, dialogue and mannerisms - and as Rifleman Moore, one of Sharpe's soldiers, he can be seen in most episodes, notably *Sharpe's Battle*, part of which Richard penned. Richard went on to serve afloat on the high seas on a square-rigged three-masted vessel as armourer / gunner on the first television series of *Hornblower*, based on the ever-popular novels of C S Forester.

Rifleman Moore's companion in crime William Spry is an altogether different character. Another of Richard's creations, Spry was born in Georgian London in 1750, and carries on a rather dubious trade, when not actively engaged in this he demonstrates all the everyday social skills of a Georgian gentleman; from lighting a candle with flint and steel, to cutting a quill pen, writing and posting a letter, dressing a wig, making tea, discussing wine, how to wear period clothes and many other recreated skills. Anyone and everyone is expected to have a go. Spry also bears an uncommon resemblance to the notorious highwayman Black Dick seen at 18th century living history events with Histrionix, and other events around England during the summer months.

Richard's period skills and background knowledge; his travels and adventures in forest and field, history and film, makes him an excellent companion for any historical exploration. He is said not just to see hard facts but also understand the tremendous struggle and suffering our ancestors have undergone and overcome as part of our colourful history.

Richard is currently a Midas Historic Tours guide for the Spanish and Portuguese battlefields of the Peninsula War, Waterloo in Belgium and The Crimean War around Sevastopol in the Ukraine. He especially loves pirates and outlaws; in 1998, he reached the zenith of his ambitions by shooting with the traditional English longbow and becoming one of Robin Hood's band of Merrie Men under the Major Oak in Sherwood Forest; where he blotted his copybook the next day in the forest by attempting at arrow-point to rob Richard the Lionheart for which he was later made to walk the plank into a nearby lake !

A keen cyclist, Richard lives - most of the time, anyway - in and around Sherwood, Nottingham.

Robin Hood; a picture-postcard, one of a series of four based on paintings by David Porter, commissioned by Ladislav Tvrdik.

Part One

Night

"Litheth, Listeneth, and holdeth thy tongue .."
from the *Tale of Gamelyn*; anon oral poem of unknown date,
recorded circa 1350

Over the years, the Legend of Robin Hood has lost nothing in the telling. Indeed, it is with the telling that the legend originated; many have since placed Robin Hood under the microscope and tried to document, explain and justify him. As the Sheriff found out, he is a very slippery and elusive character!

From the far ages and mists of antiquity he grew; some of the very first printed works in England were of him and his exploits, already well-known in stories and songs orally transmitted through a certain strata of society by those skilled in this form of entertainment. They were thought important enough to commit to precious time and paper; but before writing was even created - he was already here. What has come down to us is a memory, embellished by both fantasies and facts woven and spun into today's story of the dispossessed nobleman or stout yeoman, seeking revenge and fair play from an unjust system, finding a new home in the

*Heath Pye of the Wolfshead Bowmen in Sherwood Forest a
historical archer par excellence !*

ranks of the lowest, righting Wrongs and doing Right, struggling against adversity and oppression, finally winning through and finding love and freedom - and immortality.

The truth about a real man may never now be known, but the legend is there for all to see. The shadowy figure of Robin Hood himself stands smiling impartially today against a background of individuals and groups who rival for his favour, lay claims as to his birth, life and death; and see him - amongst other things - as a medieval knight, a bloodthirsty thief or a magical wood-elf. Trying to tie him down to one of them is as easy as finding the crock at the end of the rainbow!

We can begin to look for him in the forest, his traditional and favourite haunt.

In the dawn of Time, all men knew of Good and Bad. They sought Good and tried to avoid Bad. They made offerings to gods to secure good harvests, strong children, and continuing health to the tribe. When such things did not happen, they blamed evil spirits. That evil spirits existed, bespeaks the fact that good ones do too. In time, they were given names. The oral traditions described in detail what must and must not be done to stay on the right side of both of them, to somehow tread a path between them. Taboo was born, and associated Ritual.

One of them - the Green Man - is deeply rooted in English folklore. He goes by many names, this powerful male figure - as Lord of the Hunt, King of the Sun, Master of Fertility and Growth, striding the earth as Mother Natures consort each year, seeking Her favour and allying himself with Her. In a sacrificial death each year when he dies for us, he finds instead rebirth and secures the cycle of continuing growth for another season. Crops grow, are nurtured by the sun, are harvested, and Life goes on. He came to be worshipped and revered by the common folk. Adopted and renamed by foreign invaders such as Romans and Saxons, eclipsed in later years by Christianity, his pagan form is still remembered today by a small but growing minority of followers, a few pub signs, and the many place-names around the countryside that echo his existence.

Christianity tried to repress him. In many ways, it was impossible; he was too deeply embedded in belief. So - he was adopted by them in turn too, his memory and places of worship - the stone and the tree - built over with chapel and church, and reformed into the ceremonies we see today. But - oral tradition carried on. Despite attempts to disguise or disfigure him, the old story-tellers many wise men or village elders - renewed his memory each time they sat before a fire and performed their revered tales. The manly, lusty god who openly displayed himself proudly each year in the fertility of animals and the continuing harvest found many admirers when compared to the pious, austere, hard-hearted and unforgiving system that attempted to replace him.

He still peeps out from behind stone and tree today - and winks an eye - to those who please him by looking.

Oral traditions do not stay in a set form, despite our best efforts. Words and their meanings change; with each telling (and teller), the story changes too. Between the Norman Conquest and Caxton's printings in 1476 they have gone through many languages; Greek, Latin, French, old English, middle English and finally our English. Each left its effect on the one that succeeded it in the form of many new words and also lost ones. Story-tellers are great travellers, seeking their audience and a new story to add to their repertoire. Geoffrey Chaucer travelled extensively around Europe, writing his own stories but also collecting fresh ones. Tales also follow fashion; they would be sometimes changed deliberately by a teller to appeal to the audience in front of him, whether child or adult. Some folk tales are rooted in certain areas of the country, but have their contemporaries elsewhere. Some are about and include local heroes, who step down when the teller moves into another county, and are replaced by another more identifiable character to help the story along and gain a better understanding. Stories of dragons, gods and magic were gradually interpreted and expanded into tales of extraordinary deeds; the tales also had to compete with a formal telling of the accepted religion, which had little time for the good old days and often completely contradicted them. Storytellers were singled out for re-education, and tales of the old days began to recede into the shadows of camp and cottage firesides. Storytellers had now become hunted not by the common folk for entertainment, but by new invaders for adoption or elimination - in a struggle for the hearts and minds of the people.

By the time of the arrival of the printed word, the oral tradition of story-telling was extremely strong, not just in England but all over the world. In England, the thread of truth in belief had not been lost but it had been changed, deliberately or otherwise; persecution had made the storytellers amend tales to suit the circumstances. Many storytellers went underground and sought to keep faith - and rebel in their own way - by placing Christian priests in the stories as the bad guys, and the simple home-brewed hero of field and fable as the good guy. This cuts both ways; the old gods of stream and sky were now ostracised as evil from the pulpit, and penance paid (if you were caught) for acknowledging them. As Mother Nature receded, Father took over; the more patriarchal society became, so the penances increased in ferocity like being hanged or burned at the stake for heresy!

Who has not visualised a group of children seated cross-legged on the floor, enraptured by a storyteller skillfully practising his art? Many of us recall the Punch and Judy Man at the seaside, but few of us now can see the morals within the tale.

Storytellers have the capacity (depending on their individual skill) to tell a tale wherein is encompassed a moral. This was and still is hidden within the story. Stories of faith, chastity, hope and love are wrapped up inside Goldilocks, Cinderella and Big Bad Wolves. Instead of lecturing on a theme, it is transformed into a tale of heroes, princesses, castles and demons, instead of telling you what will become of you if you continue to be naughty, a story of what happened to someone who did (if skillfully told) will often do the trick.

In the more tolerant times of the future, it was no longer a crime to tell folktales. But in the intervening period, many of the original stories had been lost or overlapped and mixed into others. The origin of the story was lost. The establishment were happy in that the old characters in them had been successfully transformed into harmless and unbelievable buffoons, good for a laugh; or into witches and demons that mothers scared their children with as punishment if they misbehaved.

The Green Man was mixed up in all this. He began as an identifiable everyday form - visible and welcome through warm sunshine, plenty of food and drink, and the birth of birds and animals in spring; to his disappearance in autumn with the leaves on the trees and the advent of cold winter, only to return next year - and ended as some sort of demonic man-eating hobgoblin who only haunted dark places and preyed on unsuspecting humans.

The greenwood was also frequented by another character. This little character flits between the world of the living and the world of the dead. He is elusive; he cannot be caught. His childlike appearance belies the fact that he is extremely clever and cunning. He sometimes has pointed ears, dresses in green or uses a few leaves to cover himself; he is always about looking out for fun at someone else's expense. His tricks are normally simple; sometimes his plots are deep and well planned. They always resort in confusion, but with him always coming out on top and chuckling to himself. He is the original cunning little devil. Our Saxon ancestors named him *Hudekin*.

If you trip over and fall, it is he that placed the obstacle in your path. If the milk curdles, he breathed on it; if the chickens don't lay, it was he that scared them. In Ireland everyone has heard of the leprechaun; in England it was slightly different. The trickster now emerges, and has a new name; Robin Goodfellow.

Part Two

Dawn

Mundane stories of everyday life are not interesting. They bore us and do nothing for the spirit, raising no hopes. In the morning we have forgotten them. Songs and ballads follow the same rules, there are songs that can make or break the mood of the assembled party. The minstrel and bard have moved into their exalted positions of companions of Kings at court. Poetry and music are attributes which can give immortality; Kings are not slow to recognise this sort of benefit to themselves! Some great sagas of ancient history in this form survived because of their atmosphere and the skill of the story-teller; *Beowulf, Chevy Chase* and *Sir Gawaine and the Green Knight*. Rhymes and alliterations help people remember them, but sometimes the rhyme is remembered and the original meaning lost - I was listening to *Ring a ring o roses, a pocket full of posies; Atishoo, atishoo all fall down*, in the schoolyard years before I found it was a remembrance of the terrible plague of the Black Death!

Nobody wishes to be reminded of their daily struggles; we go to the theatre and the cinema today to be entertained, to escape or simply forget. The storytellers in our tale many years ago created a world that occupies the same space as us, but in a different form. It exists on a higher plane . in the world of Faery.

Everything there appears at first normal, but when examined is much larger than Life. Magic still exists there, polarised now into good and evil (although there are still quite a few grey areas) and include witches, sprites and goblins. It is linked with the everyday world and occasionally the two worlds meet; when they do, and humans are involved, they should tread carefully; their soul is now the target. The Fairies live frozen in time in or around the Underworld, in deep hollows or hills, not open to view except at certain times or by certain individuals; people lucky enough to glimpse and see them at their feasts and be invited to join them re-emerge later and although only a few minutes has passed in Faeryland, years have elapsed in their world. They have been forgotten, their families dead, their homes sold off. They have been the subject of an elaborate trick. They are only mortal; Faery is immortal, unchanged forever.

Men with dark complexions, curly black hair and grey or green eyes; men with the gift of the gab, men with extra-ordinary skills in song and dance, or with animals these are now referred to in whispers as having faery ancestry, and apart from the brown-haired or sandy-headed majority, with their brown or blue eyes. In old tales, changelings human children reputedly taken from the cradle by thieving sprites - are replaced with images, blocks of carved wood, or household objects; but they are sometimes supplanted by smaller darker babies that are alive but don't bear much resemblance to their parents. These echo the outlying areas of Olde England, places such as Wales, Scotland, Ireland and Cornwall, where the ancient darker Celtic strain is still strongest, and their

The Major Oak Team of the Wolfshead Bowmen; giving archery displays and have-a-go, also telling tales of Robin Hood daily at the Festival for eleven days in 1998

roots deepest; pushed back to the sea or contained upon an island, within a peninsula or in a mountain fastness by successive fair-haired and blue-eyed invaders with bronze and iron weapons from the east, grasping and holding the central mainland, but merely holding the borders with the old folk in their final retreats. These folk were never fully adopted or eliminated and kept many of their old traditions, including some of the darker rituals, growing stronger by bonding together in adversity. The tales of the changelings originate in the growing sexual encounters of both groups of peoples, mingling the old with the new. Before that, the old folk were seen only as fleeting shadows in a forest, or crossing the skyline on a faraway hillside; they didn't mix unless forced to do so.

I was once given a neolithic flint arrowhead found by a friend. He pointed out that such heads when found were often used as talismans by the finders; referred to as elf-arrows.

By the end of the Dark Ages, society in Britain had changed radically; beginning with simple warlike tribal bands, enduring the Roman Occupation then being left civilised but weak and open to succeeding Saxon, Danish and Viking invasions, some of whom stayed to live here; adding their own culture and beliefs to an already mixed bag. By the year 1000 the plundering raids were over, and Britain was more settled. Life was still rather uncomfortable; a fifty-year run of alternate good and bad harvests meant general starvation up to the year 1050 (although the nobles and clergy always seemed to have enough to eat). There are more people than ever before they live in villages rather than in roving tribes, each settlement connected by simple roads; a medieval equivalent of our six-lane motorways looked very similar to a modern bridleway in Sherwood. Some villages have grown into towns by the nature of their locations. People feel less isolated; communications are quicker and organised and more extensive (albeit still governed by the speed and stamina of

Modern minstrels (note hurdy-gurdy man) at the July 1998 re-opening of Nottingham Castle

the horse) but most people have never travelled outside a ten-mile radius of their home.

There are rules which govern society, and administrators who regulate them based in the larger cities, well established by 1066. The Church is well established too; their cathedrals are the most impressive buildings on earth. Monks from the great abbeys who can both read and write in a society where even kings and their advisers are sometimes illiterate are used as clerks and attorneys in the setting down on paper of laws and statutes; to reduce the amount of the religious aspects involved, young men not under holy orders are now trained and used as scribes at court. These introduce aspects known to but not readily accepted or regulated by the Church; including stories of faraway foreign lands where giants walked, and strange animals lived such as cameleopards and corkindrills, where precious stones and golden nuggets littered the earth common as the dirt, and where the one-eyed population ate their own children. That the world was flat and no-one had yet reached the edge every sane man knew to exist somewhere they did not dispute. Not yet, anyway.

Outside all this in England is the world of the field and grove, the plough and the scythe. This world still outnumbers heavily in population the more progressive world of administration and organisation nine-tenths of the population are engaged in agriculture, tied to the routine of the seasons. The Black Death Plague of the mid 1300s placed a high price on labour, and one of the causes of the Peasants Revolt of 1381. Due to the terrific drop in population, men no longer held themselves duty-bound to serve as old the price of manpower rose dramatically. The feudal system declined, despite attempts in law and decree by the ruling classes and landed gentry to retain it and fix the price, place and pace of traditional labour.

Eagles soared above Sherwood Forest in the medieval era; above the oaks, beech and birch (no sycamore-weeds, as they weren't introduced into England until the 16th century) looking down onto the peculiar practice of Sherwood of infield and outfield farming; small clearings of former grazing land enclosed by a palisade and ploughed and seeded for a few years before being returned to grazing. Over in Derbyshire, even a few grapevines clung to the uplands in a warmer climate than today, but vineyards were more popular on the southerly chalk hills of Kent.

In Laxton in Nottinghamshire, the old way of tilling the fields still goes on. Near Southwell, I shoot the longbow in a field still showing the old ridges and furrows of long ago. The system of labour in the old feudal system after AD1100 gave me the impression of an organised extortion from an immense amount of hard work with little reward from ninety-nine percent of the people for the sole benefit of less than one percent of the population; the system seemed designed to create hardship for the majority. Even simple improvements in agriculture in ones own fields was bound to a monetary payment to the feudal lord to keep your own animals on your own land to provide the fertilising manure required to improve on yield. Any improvements in animal breeding led to a requirement to produce more food, a degree of expense necessary to feed the increase in animal numbers throughout the winter, or facilitate their slaughter; somewhat negating any long-term investment.

Most of this was decreed in the past in the quaint term custom of the manor which varied from place to place (it holds the ancient origin of the term customer). The local custom of the manor which had set the former rates pre-1066 ended with the coming of the Normans after the Conquest. Rents and fees paid to the new overlords were crippling.

An increase in yield or animals would mean an increase in the tallage, set by the new overlord and to which there was no regulated form, except by the lord or his overseer's opinion of worth. Any attempt at putting tallage in writing, led to the document being interpreted and worded to suit the overlord. Even existing Saxon lords remaining on their old territory had to somehow recoup the losses incurred in buying their own lands back from the Conqueror by passing on the cost to the customer as is done today.

If a villein died, a 'heriot' was paid to his overlord in the form of the best animal or possession of the deceased; and to make things worse for the poor family the Church took the second-best too, as the mortuary fee. From one document examined, half the value of the bereaved family disappeared in payment of these customary dues.

In place of the usual customary court of a jury of the fellows of the villein in dispute, the law governing these rights were now set down on paper, by those who could both read and write the clergy, which had vested interests in financial terms and not usually serving the congregation, who invariably interpreted these matters on the behest of the landlord or their abbot. During the era 1100-1300, the numbers of those who merely represented the lord in court in any dispute as he was able pay the requisite fee more than quadrupled in number.

The entire feudal system seems to be best suited to the rapacious overlord who came into ownership of a land already well-tilled and prosperous, which he would then proceed to milk dry to suit his own greedy purposes on a short-term basis. The Church a major landowner before 1066 - seems also to have enjoyed this facility; one notorious abbot in 1280 told his villeins that they owned nothing that wasn't his by Right; except their stomachs.

The fate of many an oppressed Saxon associated with the legend of Robin Hood (Photo by kind permission of Mountfitchet Castle)

Whilst on the subject of stomachs; the diet of a poor peasant seems to have been little more than barley and oats in the form of a rough loaf, a soup or pottage made from peas, beans and onions; washed down with home-brewed ale or milk. A rare inclusion of meat seems to be either tough chicken, salt-down winter pork or a little bacon, with eggs or cheese being the basic source of protein.

The average dwelling of a serf or peasant is a small rough-built hut of wood, with the gaps filled with wattle and daub; a mixture of mud, clay and straw applied to a woven willow and hazel weave. Even the village church pre-Norman was a simple construction of the same. Simple furniture would be a chest and a bench or stools to sit on. A sack filled with straw served as a bed. The livestock were kept inside too, to prevent losses by predators, animal or human (the last wolf in England wasn't killed until AD1400, only 30 miles from Sherwood). The everyday things that are thrown away now due to bereavement kitchen utensils, pots and pans were considered important enough then to be numbered as assets in any wills. Apart from these chattels and possessions; important in a court of law; nobody thought to write of the day-to-day life and existence of the ordinary chap nobody cared and even those who could write thought it of the least importance (a common complaint these days of the modern historian trying to seek him out from old written records).

The stink of dung, sweat, animal urine and smoke from the ever-present fire in these hovels must have been over-powering. The child mortality rate was very high; a man or woman reaching the age of thirty in these conditions would have been considered - and looked - old. The poem *Piers Plowman* which we will consider later is a statement of the terrific struggle of everyday life during this era; the simple Will to Live carried people through.

A pretty nasty Man-at-Arms; the author as one of the Sheriff's Men at the Robin Hood Festival 1998

The Normans were a warlike people; when they weren't fighting a foreign enemy, they were fighting each other. If there was no-one left to fight, they went out hunting, killing animals such as wild boar, deer, hares or foxes. This hunting-killing was as much ritualised as warfare, and the sole prerogative of the nobles. To become a poacher and take the deer was to pit your wits against them and their game-keepers, and cock a snoot at this aristocratic authority but the penalties of being caught in the forest with hound or bow were terrible indeed. They would literally cut pieces of the hands and feet of you and your hound away until you were no longer physically capable of hunting; being caught with the deer itself meant death.

Anyone wishing to realise the mentality of such a race and its opportunism should read any book about the First and Second Crusades; a vast blood-lust and rape based on simple greed, masquerading under the guise of a holy quest all this before they even arrived in the Holy Land and when they eventually did, destruction and mass slaughter for gain became their standard. Life was brutal enough without these conquerors roaming the shires; there was nobody to whom the ordinary man could appeal to chastise these gangsters in their everyday practices, in custom or in court, from the year 1100 onwards. Any parish or village living under an overlord seen to be caring or trustworthy towards the lowest orders would be seen as a haven or refuge by the oppressed masses.

People travelled more, joining the traditional migrants such as tilers, masons and thatchers - when never tied to the land even under the old feudal systems; and breaking the monetary ties of out-marriages of the village - men picked up their tools, escaping slavery and sought higher wages by moving from an area where there are too many competitors to an area where there are no labouring trades. Old animosities from village or county customs are forgotten we see a rise in trade guilds, with their own taboos and rituals. The rivalry is now firmly between the common man and the ruling classes; the common man is simple, straightforward, honest. In comparison, the ruling classes are greedy, lazy, dishonest (or vice versa, depending on which side you happen to be on!). The stigma attached to serfdom (or slavery) grew strong. A power struggle is clearly about to take place. Men look for leaders to follow in these situations. In the collapse of empires or societies, a name will often be seized and held by people in the darkness and used as an inspiration and a light to find a way out of the troubles. If your faith breaks at times like this or is seen to be false, it will be replaced in the shock of discovery by another. They will be attributed sometimes even if they don't want them - with doing great deeds, speaking wisdom, having spirit, or simple freedom. They become a feature of stories and fables, perpetuated in memory and continuity. They are often identified and focused as a single person, a compilation of several features and deeds, much like the modern cinema actor who plays many popular parts and eventually becomes a conglomerate of all of them.

Memory, belief and traditions, superstitions, society upheavals and a growing gap between the classes are now being committed to paper. The ancient oral tradition is now able to be stored in a more visible, accessible - and unchangeable unless by intent - form for the growing masses able to read them. Although people steered clear of crossroads where suicides were buried for fear of the evil spirits; and also stayed away from wayside gibbets, under which were-wolves awaited human flesh to eat - they may no longer have powerfully believed in fairies as their forebears once did but they did believe in - and hoped and longed for as they squatted in their crude huts or sweated in the fields; their Freedom - and anything or anybody that would give it to them.

One man did seem to offer hope - the legend of Robin Hood was about to make an appearance, centre-stage.

Part Three

Morning

"Summer is Icumen In"
Oldest recorded English folk song

There are real men who have made the transition into faery and folklore. They can be found in history books, and their deeds recorded. There are other deeds recorded too (but not in the history books) and attributed to these same men. There are also ancient folk heroes that have also made the transition into real men, who used them perhaps as role models or simply labelled as such by the common people. Rebels, revolutionaries and freedom fighters almost always fall into this category; in death, if not in life.

Hereward the Wake fought the Normans as a Saxon outlaw after 1066 in the fens of Cambridgeshire and Norfolk. He refused to submit to conquest, and held to his oaths of loyalty. What happened to him is uncertain; he did at one time lead a small army of fellow rebels allied with the Danish fleet and captured and burned Peterborough. He may have been pardoned by William I, but later betrayed and assassinated.

Eustace the Monk although a rather dubious character fought against the established rule of law. Beginning as a monk, he left holy orders around 1190 to avenge his father's death and managed to establish himself amongst the French nobility. He fell out with them, and became an outlaw, raising a small band which grew to a band well enough established to raise a fleet and become pirates in the English Channel, based on the island of Sark. At times, he was allied both with England and France from this central position, until in 1217 as a result of becoming too involved in a baronial revolution in England, a fleet was dispatched from there, Eustace's forces were completely destroyed and Eustace himself executed by beheading on the deck of one of his own ships.

Fulk fitz Waren in 1197 succeeded his father as a Welsh border baron and pursued a claim to a nearby estate and castle in Shropshire. He lost his case, and possibly murdered the rival claimant in pique. He was outlawed but for the next three years defied and waged war on King John from his local powerbase. He was eventually pardoned, recovered the aforesaid estate and until 1215 lived in peace. He was on the side of the barons during the Magna Carta rebellion that year, lost the estate, and did not find favour with the King until 1217. He recovered the lost estate once again in 1223. Unlike the previous two, he lived on until a ripe old age, and was widely known as a wise and venerable old gentleman.

William Wallace, from circa 1296; in his monumental struggle for Scots independence against Edward I; popped up from nowhere, raised a band of loyal commoners by his example, fought for years in a guerrilla war unsupported by the officialdom he was ostensibly fighting for, and met an untimely end after a betrayal by them.

Details of these men I've used as examples can be found on paper in manuscript and roll, and are generally undisputed. But they all also feature in separate folk tales in the oral tradition - tales involving magic, strange animals, visions, dreams and prophecies and rescues of damsels in distress are associated with them; very similar to those attributed to our Robin Hood. Some of their bad attributes are reduced or omitted, and their good qualities are magnified. There are also other tales which pre-dated their activities, and less well-known; some of which reflect traditions in Nordic sagas, brought over by the Danes and Vikings in an earlier age but mingled with the later tales from other cultures. One of these feature Odin / Wotan in his earthly disguise as Grimnir; which I was told when translated means "the hooded one". But why aren't these real men today as well-known as our Robin Hood? [*1]

Illiteracy is still the norm amongst over three-quarters of the population; the oral tradition still holds strong. The Old King Cole of the popular nursery rhyme is another character, originating in the Dark Ages. How many thinking of Santa Claus or Father Christmas know he was in one reality a bishop of Greek descent living in Myra, Turkey?

Robin Hood is found on printed paper in five ballads and a play, between 1450 and 1500. Early printers placed the ballads on paper for all to see, derived and written down from the oral ballads of an earlier date. In 1377, a poem by Langland entitled *Piers Plowman* about the common mans struggle was written down and mentions Robin Hood in a commonplace manner, fully expecting the reader to know who he is; other evidence takes him earlier still, into the middle of the thirteenth century.

Robin Hood was established and in common knowledge by the year 1300. He lived in a forest, with other outlaws, used a longbow to shoot the King's deer, and robbed people on the highway. He didn't, by reading the early ballads, know any Maid Marian, wasn't a disgruntled or dispossessed nobleman, doesn't shoot an arrow from his death bed, doesn't enjoy any sort of blind admiration from his men, or even rob from the Rich in order to give to the Poor. The earliest ballads also

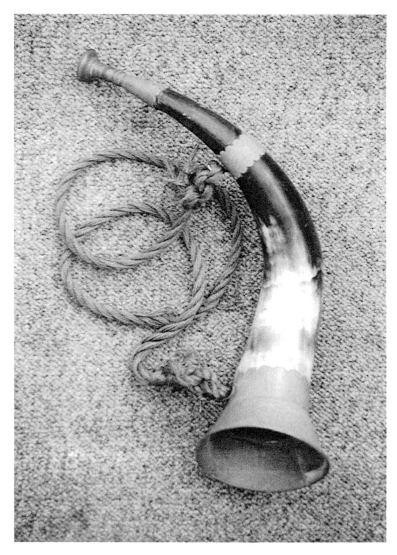

A traditional hunting horn; Robin Hood blew one of these three times to summon his band of merry men. This one was made by the author for use at the 14th Robin Hood Festival at Edwinstowe in 1998.

don't mention his real name or why he was outlawed, Little John being a giant, or Friar Tuck.

But they do now.

These aspects of the legend grew since 1450, when the oral tales were committed at that stage of their development on paper but continued to change and grow; and due to popular success lead to the printing of more of them, in which new characters and adventures were introduced. This is not to say that there may have been oral tales that were not committed to paper, but were still pretty widely known. The ones that have survived in ballad form are in some cases incomplete, start and end abruptly and read as a mix-match of several assorted tales grouped together; they also stand misinterpretation from the old English language into the new. These ballads form most of the solid evidence used by the modern Robin-hunters to pin down his existence, livelihood and origins to specific persons, times and places; and they have been debated and picked-over for many years. Because of their ambiguities, they can be interpreted to prove almost anything to anyone; their language and historical content have been said to show they were written down somewhere between 1350 and 1450; and in 1450 after a little editing, patching and gluing to suit they began to be printed on machines for general consumption. These tales may have been copied or edited from older ballads; they too in turn taken from even older notes taken at oral recitations of even older stories from earlier historical periods. Some of them still read in the fashion of a previous oral poem.

Two Scots historians of between 1400 and 1440, placed Robin Hood on record as having existed between 1260 and 1280. Another writing in 1520, placed him firmly in the year 1193-4 at the time Richard I The Lionheart was imprisoned in Germany following the crusades. Nobody ever wrote down that they had known him, or even wrote of anyone who had said they had known him or seen him. But that he actually existed, the three historians do not dispute; only his time and place are argued.

The legend by the year AD1500 is hence well-established. Robin is a stout yeoman who lives in the woods with a band of fellow outlaws, is supported by the local population and has many adventures in which his skill at arms or cunning strategy always leaves him with the upper hand. He is not above the Law; he is the law; or at least his interpretations of it. But at that time the legend hadn't stopped growing - even today, a modern story-teller here disclosed to me how Robin gained most of his success; he was taught by forest mystics who could talk to the trees themselves and was given secrets and advice by the ancient fellow forest-dwellers, elves and fairies.

By AD1700, he had in popular belief a birthplace, a family tree and many places named after him even his gravesite and those of his companions had been discovered and chronicled. There are now even more ballads, adding fresh characters and exploits.

From AD1800, each year in each spring, Robin Hood - clad in his lincoln-green clothes, bow in hand and blowing his hunting-horn left the dark forest and embarked on fresh adventures; but now he left a clearer trail for his future seekers to follow.

Footnote
1. In deference to any Scots reader, I cannot do William Wallace the justice here he deserves in the space permitted. He is perhaps unique in having made the transition from real man to folklore and then back again (mostly through the media of recent cinema, the Devolution process and the SNP).

He is also attributed with magical qualities mostly through the writings of one contemporary and enigmatic poet many of whose tales of Wallace were well-known during Wallace's own lifetime. He is worth a guidebook on his own - I would advert the reader to a publication new to the bookshelves on Wallace which explains his birth, life and death in great detail. The other three men cited are also dealt with in more detail in the book Outlaws of Medieval England by Maurice Keen.

The new statue to Robin and Marian in Edwinstowe village

Part Four

The Ballads and Stories of Robin Hood

> *Once upon a time*
> Traditional beginning to all fairy stories

The early stories all have underlying themes - the Sheriff is seen to be the bad guy, representing local authority; church officials are seen to be rather greedy characters, looking to their own pockets rather than care for their flocks; Little John and Robin are often at loggerheads with Robin coming over as a rather headstrong young man on several occasions; Robin fights - at the drop of a hat sometimes - some quite doughty opponents, who invariably defeat him; Robin saves face only by the outcome of the story being that the winner of the combats join his band and accept him as leader.

Some of the stories sound very implausible; some for continuity's sake omit realities of time and place. The outlaws always live in an apparent atmosphere of plenty, and no evidence is ever seen of any of the obviously existing hardships; perhaps obscured behind opening hints of an idyllic woodland existence complete with birdsong.

Various clues have always been highlighted in the stories, such as monetary rates, prices for goods, customs and names of people and places as evidence to try to fix a historical framework for Robin's existence. These could of course have been amended successively at the time of writing / printing the story by successive authors to make the story ring true for their particular audience. I do recommend the reader to try and read the stories in their original ballad forms [*1]. I have ended each story with a few observations on their content for the reader to think about, with a concluding part about how far you can see inside the stories.

A dozen stories follow and are included here only as examples of how the legend got started in print and the foundation for its evolution; the reader can compare them with the established story today. They may have a common root but today have countless branches!

There are many more stories but many have been unrecorded and hence forgotten; and they have been replaced by many new ones. Collecting old storybooks which contain them is a large part of the interest in modern Robin Hood memorabilia [*2].

Robin Hood and the Monk

This is one of the earliest surviving and longest stories about Robin Hood. It is said to be doubtful as whether it was ever set to music, and remained an oral recital. It contains the elements of adventure - betrayal of trust, cunning, swash-buckling, murder, a turning-of-the-tables, the defeat of the evil Sheriff and a final reconciliation between the two main hero-characters. It also reveals part of the darker side of Robin Hood, and begins to bring Little John out from Robin's shadow to stand as an equally important character in the growing legend.

The story begins in the greenwood, with a merry atmosphere of early summer; as it is Easter, little John is talking to Robin about the joys of Spring. Robin is in a dismal mood, suffering from not being able to go to Mass for over a fortnight. Probably as a result of John's emanations, he decides he will go to church in Nottingham that very day. Much advises him to take along himself and twelve of the outlaw band for protection. Robin declines, saying he will go with John alone who will carry his bow. John suggests they play a game for small stakes along the way to pass the time (and possibly lighten Robins bad mood); in doing so he wins five shillings, which Robin denies - he finally strikes Little John in the ensuing argument and in a worsening mood. Little John draws his sword; saying if it were not the fact that he has accepted Robin as his leader, he would have struck him down. He then leaves to go his own way, leaving Robin - and his bad temper - to continue alone.

Robin arrives at St Mary's church, and kneels to pray. He is recognised as an outlaw by a monk there, who he has formerly robbed of the large sum of one hundred pounds. The monk goes quickly goes to the Castle and reports the fact to the Sheriff, who goes out to catch Robin, spurred on by the monk.

Robin is surprised at mass inside the church; he draws a double-handed sword and attacks the Sheriff's men. His sword breaks on the Sheriff's helmet, and he is taken prisoner.

Later, the news arrives in Sherwood that Robin is taken. The band are much distressed the news is discussed; a plan to waylay the monk who is getting ready to ride to London the next day to seek an execution warrant for Robin swings into action. Little John and Much will ambush the monk, leaving the rest of the band to look after the camp, fearful of a move by the Sheriff to capture or break up the rest of the band now he has their leader.

From a house near the road, they wait for the monk to leave the castle after collecting the letter from the Sheriff to the King. When they see him, attended by a page, they leave to meet them. John falls in with the monk, asking him for news of the capture of the famous outlaw. The monk tells all, unsuspecting, and agrees to let John and Much escort them part of the way after hearing that they too were robbed by Robin Hood and have no reason to like him.

When they are clear of the town in a lonely spot, John pulls the monk off his horse; he draws his sword and swipes off his head Much then kills the page in the spirit of 'dead men tell no tales'. The two outlaws then search the monk for the letter, hide the bodies in the undergrowth, and set off to see the King in the place of the monk and his page.

The King is glad that Robin has been taken; he asks John and Much to become official messengers after they say the monk unfortunately died on the way down to London and asked them to deliver the letter to the King. He commands John and Much to take a message back to the Sheriff to deliver up Robin to him for punishment, and pays them each for doing so.

Back at Nottingham Castle, Will Scarlet and members of the band have been harassing the garrison by shooting arrows into the Castle. The castle is hence sealed tight when John and Much arrive after dark, but they are let in by the porter when they show the Kings Seal on their message. The Sheriff receives them at once, but asks after the monk he sent to the King; John states the King was so pleased at the news he has made the monk Abbot of Westminster and bidden him to take up his duty at once - he hints at a reward from the King for the Sheriff too! The Sheriff declares a celebration, invites John and Much and all there get roaring drunk. As the Sheriff falls asleep dead-drunk, John and Much who have secretly stayed sober - slip away down to the dungeons. John calls out that the outlaw has escaped, and watches which cell the jailer goes to check - John then pins the jailer to the stone wall with his sword, removes his keys from his body and lets Robin out of jail. John gives Robin the jailer's sword, and they escape from the castle into the town by dropping over the castle walls where they are lowest.

Early next day, the jailer is found dead. The alarm is sounded throughout the castle and town, but the outlaw has already gone far into Sherwood Forest. The Sheriff rages; he fears the King's anger when he finds out the outlaw has escaped his writ and declares that anyone who catches Robin Hood shall have a good reward in return.

Back at camp in Sherwood, Little John tells Robin he has done him a good turn for a bad one - referring to the blow from Robin Hood that he was given. Robin and John settle their quarrel; at first, Robin suggests that John should become their new leader, but John will have none of it - he wants to stay just where he is. They all celebrate with a woodland feast.

Back at the castle, the Sheriff hears the news that the King is mightily angry with him, and has said the Sheriff should be hanged for his failure. The King also states that Little John is a very clever fellow, having beguiled not just the Sheriff but him too, in loyalty to his 'adopted' master John loves Robin Hood more than he does his King - and despite John's actions, admires his bold spirit.

Notes

Robin and John argue over sportsmanship; it comes to blows. Is Robin basically a bad-tempered and headstrong young man? Or does his behaviour reflect his desperate need to go to mass and pray? Such behaviour and the significance of other examples of medieval religious fervour was liked by an acquaintance of mine to a modern sense as being similar to an over-reliance on hard drugs; Robin's impetuosity in his dealings with John occur in other stories too, outside of any religious context. Is John seen often as the older and wiser man - over-protective of Robin, because of his youth? This same acquaintance gave another suggested explanation for it which I refuse to print here.

Robin is praying inside church apparently still fully-armed. In other tales, the fight takes place outside the church when Robin attempts to leave.

There were no dungeons in Nottingham Castle as such but important prisoners were detained or incarcerated in many of the castle rock caves (see Parts Seven and Eight in this book).

Robin Hood and the Potter

A delightful tale, with cunning and trickery playing a large part in it. The story includes a fight, a disguise, a fair lady, a bold ruse and all ending happily ever after; except for the Sheriff of course!

Once again, the scene is set in the greenwoods; Robin Hood is also described in a surrounding of greenery as courteous, fair, free, a stout yeoman devoted to the Virgin Mary so none of the listeners or readers are in any doubt as to his status from the start.

Robin Hood, Little John and other outlaws are out watching a road through the forest. They see the approach of a potters cart Robin and John both recognise him; Robin as someone who has never paid him his toll for using the road through his forest as often as he does; and Little John as he has been beaten by the potter in a fight with staves. John warns Robin the potter is a stout fighter; Robin bets John forty shillings he can best him. The money is left with one of the outlaws, and the fun begins.

Robin steps out into the road and challenges the potter; the potter refuses to pay any such toll, and tells Robin to clear off or he will give him a sound beating. Robin demands again he pay the toll, and tells the potter he is none other than Robin Hood himself. At this, the potter grasps his quarterstaff from within the cart and leaps onto the road - Robin draws sword and buckler, and the fight begins.

John prevents the outlaws still hidden in the bushes to laugh or interfere; he tells them the potter will fight well, and it should be entertaining. The potter knocks Robin's buckler from his hand, then deals a heavy blow to the outlaw's neck, dropping him to the ground.

At this, the outlaws emerge from cover to prevent the potter from possibly finishing Robin off. Robin is still on the ground, dazed. Little John bends over Robin as he starts to come round and asks him if he has conceded the bet? Robin states that even if it had been a hundred shillings, the money is John's without a doubt!

Robin is helped up; he speaks to the potter, and tells him that he will never be stopped on the road for the toll by him again, even if he comes along it every day! They make their peace, and Robin offers the potter his friendship; he suggests they change clothes and Robin will go into Nottingham instead to sell the potter's wares from the cart. Although Little John and the outlaws try to persuade Robin from this, Robin decides he will do it. The potter agrees as he considers himself a sports-man too, and a self-confessed fine fellow to boot!

Robin drives the cart to Nottingham market square, where he draws a lot of attention as he begins to sell them at ridiculously low prices. Before all his stock was snapped up by the good folk of Nottingham, he sent some of the finest pots to the Sheriff's wife at her home. She is overjoyed with the gift, and invites Robin to come and meet her husband. They all sit down to eat a lunch of bread, ale and wine. Two of the Sheriff's men begin to discuss a wager concerning archery, of forty shillings to win by hitting a marker at a certain distance. Robin states he can do it; the Sheriff's men try, but fail. Robin then selects an arrow and hits the marker, breaking it into three pieces.

The Sheriff asks Robin where he learned to shoot arrows Robin astounds the Sheriff by saying with Robin Hood. The Sheriff asks the potter if he knows where Robin Hood is; to which the potter says he does, and agrees to take the Sheriff there with a party of men next day. Robin thanks the Sheriff's wife for her kindness, and gives her a gold ring to wear as a remembrance of him.

When deep in the greenwood next day, the potter blows his hunting horn; a crowd of outlaws appear, led by Little John. The Sheriff and his men are quickly surrounded. John jocularly asks Robin if he has sold all his pots, to which Robin replies he was so successful he has brought the Sheriff along to meet them. He then relieves the miserable Sheriff of his purse, which is found to contain a hundred pounds. The Sheriff is sent back to Nottingham after being stripped of clothes and all the soldiers gear; Robin warns him that if it were not for the fact he has a loving wife, he would have killed him. He sends the Sheriff back to Nottingham with a white pony as a gift for the Sheriff's wife from Robin Hood.

The tale ends with the potter being generously over-paid for his pots from the Sheriff's purse by Robin Hood; back in Nottingham the Sheriff's wife laughs it all off, saying that the Sheriff was duped by a very charming and clever man, and got nothing at all from the encounter except to lose face, his clothes and his soldiers equipment - and also pay ten times over for the pots Robin Hood gave her for nothing!

The story ends under the greenwood tree, with the narrator asking for Gods mercy on Robin Hoods soul and all good yeomanry.

Notes
Robin and John arguing again; albeit this time with a bit of humour, for money. Robin is still headstrong by taking on the potter despite everyone's advice. Robin may be seen to wish to bounce back and suggest another adventure as a result of him getting the worst from the previous one in the front of all his men!

In a very similar story, Robin meets a butcher instead of the potter and the same thread runs through the tale; the Sheriff is astonished that he sells his meat so cheap at market when it is scarce Robin tells him he has access to an unlimited quantity, and the Sheriff goes off with him to see and hopes to buy it from the young man - the trick is revealed when Robin shows the Sheriff the herd of Royal deer in Sherwood Forest; the Sheriff loses the three hundred pounds he has brought to buy the cheap meat, and is then packed off back to his wife in Nottingham.

A Lytell Geste of Robin Hood

This tale contains most of the grist of the established legend. It was also probably more popular than any of the others; undergoing a few small changes in each printing. It may contain three separate stories, linked together into one epic tale trying to put a simple and complete life and times of Robin Hood before the audience or reader;

Robin Hood and the Poor Knight
Robin Hood and the Sheriff of Nottingham
Robin Hood and the King

It also deals with the death of Robin Hood at the ending of the story.

The story begins with Robin Hoods meeting with Sir Richard of the Lea in the greenwood, after Robin has decreed he wishes to have a guest to eat dinner with the band. Little john, accompanied by Will Scarlet and Much, meet and waylay Sir Richard on the road. Sir Richard accepts their invitation to dine, and the group return to Robin Hoods camp. In the course of events, Sir Richard's story comes out - he cannot offer to pay for his dinner as he has only a scant purse on his person; he is travelling abroad to seek his fortune as he cannot repay a debt due to his son having accidentally killed a knight in a tournament. He has mortgaged his lands as surety for the debt to the abbot of St Mary's. Robin is impressed with the old knight, and offers to loan him the £400. At first the old knight feels he cannot accept, as he has no collateral to offer and doubts his ability to repay it, except by his sworn word on the Virgin Mary. This is good enough for Robin Hood; he gives the knight the money, and also re-equippes him with new clothes, a horse, a good saddle, new harness, boots and spurs. Little John is also asked to attend him as his squire.

The company set off for St Mary's; where the abbot despite a plea from the prior and advised by a cellarer (having the duties of a sort of butler and steward) and a justice to whom he has paid a fee, decides Sir Richard is not coming and will foreclose and seize his lands. Sir Richard arrives, still wearing his old clothes; at first he asks for clemency on his knees, saying he cannot raise the sum in the time given. The abbot and the justice declare they will seize his lands. At that point, Sir Richard throws down the £400 given to him by Robin

Hood, and leaves for home. Much to the abbot's dismay, he leaves as the cellarer and justice then refuse to give the abbot back their fees. Little John returns to the greenwood to report on the proceedings.

Now there is a long pause in time, but not in the story itself.

Some time later, Sir Richard manages to collect enough money to repay the loan; he sets off with a large retinue of men to meet Robin in Barnsdale. Robin Hood is a little disappointed that Sir Richard has not yet appeared to repay the debt on the appointed day; unknown to him, Sir Richard has been delayed due to rescuing a man at a wrestling match. Once again, Robin sends out Little John, Much and Will Scarlet to seek a dinner guest. They meet a high-ranking monk with a body of fifty-two men. They put this group to flight, and take the monk back to Robin, who turns out to be the very same cellarer of St Mary's. After he is fed and watered, he is asked how much money he has in order to pay for the dinner. At first the cellarer states he has only 20 marks, but Little John finds 800 in his baggage. Robin jocularly declares that the Virgin Mary has seen fit to repay the loan twice over, and keeps all the money. The cellarer is then dispatched from the camp.

Sir Richard then appears. Robin tells him he considers the debt already repaid, and gives the knight £400 of the booty to buy another fresh horse and equipment.

The Second Story

The outlaw band is now set further in the south. Little John takes part in an archery contest and impresses the Sheriff of Nottingham with his skill. The Sheriff tells him he wishes to offer him a job in his service; at first, John gives a false name and declines as he claims to be already in another knights service - Sir Richard - but accepts the Sheriff's offer to serve for one year. He serves as a huntsman, but one day instead of going out with the Sheriff he stays in bed and sleeps late. When he wakes, he demands breakfast from the Castle cook; the cook quarrels with him, and a sword fight ensues. Little John is impressed with the cook's skill he persuades him to join the outlaw band. They set off together into Sherwood, taking a good deal of the Sheriff's silver tableware with them in a sack, which they drop off at camp. Little John sets off to seek the Sheriff, and finds him hunting. He tells him a story of how he has spotted a fine hart, the Sheriff agrees to follow him; Little John leads him into an ambush, where the Sheriff is taken prisoner by Robin Hood. The Sheriff is forced to eat dinner in the outlaws camp off his own stolen plates, then forced to say he will not pursue or punish the outlaws for their trick in exchange for being set free.

The Sheriff is now furious. He breaks his promise made under duress and tries to trap the outlaws in another archery contest in Nottingham. This time it is he who sets the ambush, and the outlaws are shot at and attacked after leaving the contest; Little John is wounded by an arrow in the knee, and things look grim. Robin Hood refuses to leave Little John, and they set off, hotly pursued by the Sheriff's men to take shelter in Sir Richard's castle nearby. Despite the Sheriff's protests, Sir Richard gives shelter to the outlaws. The Sheriff declares he will send a message to the King; he also leaves two men to watch the castle.

These two men capture Sir Richard whilst he is out alone, hawking; Robin and the group have already returned to the forest. Upon hearing the news of his capture from Sir Richard's wife, Robin decides to rescue Sir Richard from Nottingham Castle. A small army of outlaws goes into Nottingham they confront the Sheriff and his men, who have brought out Sir Richard as a hostage. Robin shoots the Sheriff with an arrow, then cuts off his head; the rest of the outlaws also draw their swords and attack the garrison, driving them off. Robin declares the Sheriff evil, and only the King himself can put things to rights. This done, they all leave Nottingham and return to Sherwood Forest to await proceedings.

The Third Story

The King is angry at the Sheriff when he receives the news; he decides to go north to Nottingham and capture Robin Hood and Sir Richard himself. Wisely asking advice and asking for information, he decides to take the advice of a forester and go into the greenwoods in disguise. He adopts the disguise of an abbot, and takes five of his best knights along too disguised as monks. Robin Hood himself surprises the King and his men; they are relieved of their money - £40 but half is given back in return for the abbot telling the truth. The abbot now declares he has a message for Robin from the King himself they agree to go to the outlaw camp and eat a feast, and then the abbot can deliver his message in more comfortable surroundings. After the feast, there is an archery contest. Robin Hood shoots well at first but finally misses the mark (maybe after too much ale and wine). The King strikes him a blow as a punishment. Robin then recognises the King as a result of the power of the blow. He professes his loyalty to the Crown, and begs the Kings forgiveness.

The King pardons Robin and the outlaw band, on the condition that they leave the woods and serve him at Court. This they agree to, and all dressed in Lincoln-green they leave to return to Nottingham the next day, playing games and sports along the way.

The story ends with Robin becoming bored at Court; the rest of the pardoned outlaws have already left to return to their homes. After only fifteen months, Robin decides to leave too. The King grants him a weeks leave, but Robin once back in the woods decides to stay there forever rather than return to the Kings service.

The story ends rather abruptly with Robin Hood - now an old man - going off to Kyrkesley twenty-two years later where he is betrayed for no apparent reason by Roger of Doncaster and the prioress during his medical treatment, and finally dies.

A short epitaph to the story asks Christ to bless Robins soul, as although an outlaw he did poor men much good.

Notes
The story still doesn't say why Robin is an outlaw. Some quick addition reveals he spent thirteen years as an outlaw in the greenwood before being reconciled with the King; he spends a year and a half at Court, before returning to the greenwood for another twenty-two years living in peace. These two figures combined give Robin a speculatory age of high teens or early twenties at the start of his career as folk-outlaw at the beginning of the Geste.

The Death of Robin Hood (1)

In the oldest account of this story, it is Church Lees that Robin goes to for medical attention; in another Kirkesley Priory, and in another Kirkley Hall. In one printing in the seventeenth century, the epitaph to Robin Hood attributed to the grave at Kirklees was included at the end which came first is still uncertain. There were several other changes which took place in this story as it was retold and reprinted the inclusion of Robin's hunting horn call, the arrow sent to mark his grave and the dropping of the witch-woman warning Robin of his impending doom, and the overall grim and gloomy atmosphere. There may be several parts still missing from the two existing examples of the story on paper.

The death of Robin is alluded to at the end of the *Lytell Geste* - but in this story is given a much more detailed account. Robin's death is also recounted in a different form in *Robin Hood and the Valiant Knight* (see later).

What isn't said in the way of an introduction is that by the time of his death, Robin Hood has been living back in the woods for twenty-two years after being pardoned for his past crimes by the King but having left the Court through boredom. Robin is now an old man; he is failing fast, and wishes to go to seek medical aid for what he sees as an internal disorder.

One story begins enigmatically and ambiguously in unknown surroundings with Robin making this fact plain to the remaining members of the outlaw band. Will Scarlet speaks up and warns Robin it is not safe to go without a strong escort of fifty men. He alludes to a powerful man in the area who has a score to settle with Robin Hood, and would kill him if he could. Despite this advice, Robin states he will go accompanied by Little John alone, for both speed and secrecy.

They set off; making good time, except when crossing a stream of black water by a plank bridge where an old woman is kneeling, crying and cursing the name of Robin Hood. What happens here is uncertain (a part may be missing from the story at this point but other tales tell of the wise-woman telling Robin to beware a curse laid on him that although he has invariably defeated men by always being faithful to the Virgin Mary, it will be by a woman's hand that he finally meets his doom).

The two men continue their journey after recounting that the Prioress a female - is family to Robin Hood, and will certainly do him no harm when they meet. They quickly get to their journeys end; they are admitted by the prioress herself, to whom Robin makes himself known and gives her a sum of money for their keep. The two men apparently rest for a while, with Red Roger at some point arriving at the place in the background.

The prioress takes Robin to a place of safety, and bids him partly undress ready for the treatment. She cuts through a vein, and Robin begins to bleed. The prioress leaves the room, and once outside meets Little John who asks her how Robin is? She answers that he is not well, and badly needing quiet and rest; persuading Little John not to wait by his bedside as he wishes, but to leave him to sleep.

Robin Hood eventually (in one story by a dream) suspects betrayal; he draws his sword from nearby and hides it under the coat covering his legs just as Red Roger enters the room carrying a sword. Robin - weak from loss of blood - tries to reach a window and call for help, but Roger stabs him in the side. Robin with a great effort slashes Roger through the neck with the previously unseen weapon; Roger falls and Robin states he will be fed to the dogs for his guilt. Little John arrives after hearing the noise, and Robin falls into his arms. Robin asks Little John to first bless him and give him what absolution he can so he can die in peace; then to take him up, and bury his body in the woods with his weapons by his side.

Another later version of the same story takes Robin off to see his cousin the prioress after feeling his age when shooting against Little John, for the same bleeding and hopeful rejuvenation. On the way, he is taken ill and has to stop somewhere for a while, when Robin and Little John arrive eventually at Kirkley Hall, the prioress is ready and waiting for him. She agrees to treat him, and takes him off to a room where she opens a vein and locks him in. Robin by the next day is so weak he can hardly move; he manages to reach his hunting horn and blows three great blasts. Little John hears the call nearby, and races to help Robin. He smashes his way into the place, and reaches the dying Robin. Little John asks

Robin to let him burn the place down in return for the prioress' treachery but Robin states he has never harmed a woman, and will not start now. He asks Little John to ready his bow so he can shoot a final arrow from the room into the woods, and where it falls to bury him.

The story ends with an epitaph almost identical to the one at the Kirklees gravesite.

ROBERT EARL OF HUNTINGTON
LIES UNDER THIS LITTLE STONE
NO ARCHER WAS LIKE HIM SO GOOD
HIS WILDNESS NAMED HIM ROBIN HOOD
FULL THIRTEEN YEARS AND SOMETHING MORE
THESE NORTHERN PARTS HE VEXED SORE
SUCH OUTLAWS AS HE AND HIS MEN
MAY ENGLAND NEVER KNOW AGAIN.

Notes
There is a similarity about Red Roger's death and that of Guy of Gisborne; both adversaries just manage to snatch defeat from the jaws of victory in fighting and wound Robin Hood by stabbing him in the side; this also leads to comparison to the stab wound Jesus Christ received whilst on the Cross.

Robin Hood and the Valiant Knight (2)

A much later version of the *Death of Robin Hood*. This tale, written sometime in the seventeenth century, enjoyed a brief resurrection in the eighteenth century before apparently plummeting into obscurity.

The tale opens at the King's court - Robin Hood has been enjoying too mush success and popular support; the bishops and nobles have all advised the King that he must be taken to avoid anarchy and potential revolution amongst the population. A knight named Sir William is given command of a hundred stout archers, told to put on his shining armour and go forth, serve the Royal Warrant and capture the outlaw before he causes any more trouble.

This Sir William duly does; the force march up to the greenwood, where Sir William calls a halt. He will go forward alone and serve the warrant if Robin Hood surrenders in the face of the heavy opposition, then there needn't be a battle. When Sir William finds Robin relaxing in a tent, he serves the papers on him. Robin reads them, then asks why he should consider any surrender as he has a hundred and fifty men of his own, all equally well-armed and good fighters? Sir William then tries to seize Robin and take him prisoner, but Robin is warned by William Locksley and Sir William fails in the attempt. Robin blows his hunting-horn to summon his men; Sir William retreats to summon his men also. Both forces are now drawn up in battle-order; the archers let fly, and the fighting begins. Sir William falls to the first arrow flights, and is killed. After four hours, the battle ends with both forces retiring; the archers back to London, and the outlaws back into the forest. Robin however is taken suddenly ill, he sits by a tree and allows a monk to bleed him *3; which eventually kills him. As soon as the rest of the outlaws realise their leader is dead, they flee; some overseas to Flanders, France and Spain. Eventually they drifted back to England.

The story ends with why it was possibly written; the epitaph which the reader here you have, upon his grave - at Kirklees.

ROBERT EARL OF HUNTINGDON
LIES HERE HIS LABOUR BEING DONE NO ARCHER
LIKE HIM WAS SO GOOD
HIS WILDNESS NAMED HIM ROBIN HOOD
FOR THIRTEEN YEARS AND SOMEWHAT MORE
THESE NORTHERN PARTS HE VEXED SORE

Notes

The epitaph on the grave at Kirklees is unreadable today as Irish navvies, believing the stone to cure toothache, chipped bits off in the nineteenth century after reading that Robin Hood came to Kirklees for a miracle cure too! The epitaph can be taken to be a compliment or an admonition depending on how it is spoken.

It is possible that the William Locksley of the tale - who in it warns Robin and very little else - is the beginning of the attachment to Robin of the title Locksley. By 1640, a dale just outside Sheffield was known as the birthplace of Robin Hood, but became wider known as such after the publication of Sir Walter Scott's *Ivanhoe* in 1820. Will Scarlet is said to be Robin's nephew in later tales; who better to warn him of treachery in this story after his death at the hands of his aunt in the earlier tale than another blood-relative?

Robin Hood and Guy of Gisborne

This again is possibly a written remnant of an older incomplete oral tale, as several parts of the remaining evidence are missing or incomplete too; such as the details of Robin's nightmare, why Guy is out looking for Robin in the first place, and how Robin Hood knows of the capture of Little John and the need to rescue him and where, which he does using the disguise of Guy; and what happens to Will Scarlet and the rest of the band who are chased off by the Sheriff's posse. Again, a darker side is shown of Robin Hood after his victory over Guy.

The story ends rather abruptly with John taking centre-stage by killing the Sheriff with an arrowshot. The whole story reads like a bad dream in itself.

The ballad once more begins by setting the scene of the greenwood, complete with birdsong. Robin and Little John are there; they are discussing a dream that Robin has had previously. John declares that they are but passing fancies; but Robin is troubled. He suggests they go out and seek the two knights that Robin has dreamed will appear to him, beat him and tie him up.

They see at some distance a man leaning on a tree, clad in a horse-hide coat still complete with head, tail and mane; he also has a bow, arrows, sword and dagger - and looks like he knows how to use them. John suggests he goes and talks to the man, whilst Robin stays hidden. Robin, in a temper, says he does not allow his men to risk themselves for him at any time, nor has ever done so he threatens that if it were not risking breaking his bow, he would strike Little John with it for the suggestion. Once again, they quarrel, John leaves Robin and strides off into the woods.

The story now briefly shifts; John arrives in Barnsdale to find two of the outlaw band dead, and sees Will Scarlet running for his life pursued by 140 men and the Sheriff himself. John attempts to defend Will; he looses an arrow which kills one of the Sheriff's men (William of Trent) but the bow breaks. Six of the Sheriff's men attack Little John and take him - they tie him to a tree; meanwhile Will escapes, still pursued by many of the Sheriff's men.

Robin meanwhile has studied the man; he approaches him. They wish each other Good-day, and set to talking. Guy tells Robin he appears to be an archer, perhaps a forester, he is seeking a forest guide in his attempt to find Robin Hood. They agree to shoot at the wand, to test each other's skill at an amazing range of 60 rods (330 yards). Guy is bested by Robin, and Guy finally asks Robin his name, to which Robin replies Guy should say his first.

Guy states he is a soldier of fortune and a bounty-hunter, living nowhere in particular; his born name is Guy of Gisborne. Robin then states that he lives in the greenwood; and his name is Robin Hood. Both men draw swords and begin to fight; for two hours they parry and thrust, slash and slice Robin stumbles on a tree root, and Guy stabs him in the left side with his sword. Robin prays to the Virgin Mary for help. he leaps up, and in a wild stroke with his sword he mortally wounds Guy, who falls.

Robin cuts off Guy's head, and sets it on the end of his longbow. He then draws his knife and slashes the face until it is unrecognisable, leaving it by the tree. Robin then strips Guys body; he takes off his coat of lincoln-green, throwing it over Guy's remains, and puts on Guy's horse-hide coat. He also puts on Guy's gear, including his sword and hunting horn, from which he blows a loud mort.

The Sheriff hears the mort; he declares it a pre-arranged signal - Robin Hood is dead, killed by Guy. Robin then appears from nearby, clad in Guy's horse-hide; the Sheriff takes him for Guy.

The Sheriff is flushed with success; he asks Guy what reward he will have. Guy asks for no monetary reward, but having killed the master he will now kill the slave. The Sheriff is astonished - he says Guy might have had a good reward, but as he asks to kill Little John, so shall it be instead. Little John has recognised Robin's voice; he readies himself for the coming trick.

Robin moves towards Little John, telling the Sheriff and his men to stand back and leave him to hear the outlaw's last words and do the job alone; Robin then whips out his knife and cuts Little John free, thrusting Guy's bow and arrows into his hands. They turn and face the Sheriff's men; the Sheriff turns and begins to ride off towards Nottingham followed by his men. Little John nocks and arrow and takes aim his arrow takes the Sheriff through the back into the heart, and he is killed.

Notes

Once again, the enmity between Robin and John emerges. Little John takes his leave, after past encounters; his loyalty comes and goes with Robin's moods.

The action is set in Barnsdale - but the Sheriff heads back to Nottingham.

Guy is probably a bounty-hunter, although no pre-reward is stated, except for the taken understanding that the 'Sheriff' will pay up due to previous offers. The price on Robin's head must by now be steadily growing.

Guy's costume may reflect those worn by mummers in folk-dances; other than that, horsehide is a grand leather for protection against the elements.

It is John who shoots the Sheriff; in another later story, to avenge the death of Will Scarlet in the initial ambush. William of Trent is killed in this same ambush, but his passing is then regretted by the author.

Why does Robin take the dead Guy by the hair and cut off his head? Why then mutilate Guy's face after sticking the head on the end of a bow? He must have known of Guy - or Guy's reputation - before they finally meet; or it is more evidence of Robin's bad temper this time becoming battle-fury. Mutilation of dead enemy corpses is known in several primitive cultures;

in some cases they are eaten by the victors for them to absorb the courage of the defeated enemy. Celtic culture contains a distinct head-hunting aspect.

In a more modern tale, Guy has previously insulted Maid Marian; Robin could be seen to be taking revenge for that insult.

You can't see a wand at 330 yards; the odds for splitting it must be tremendous! Again, a little exaggeration to make the character seem larger-than-life.

Robin Hood and the Jolly Pinner of Wakefield

The pinner in the story (a pinfold was a corral or enclosure where stray animals were placed until their owners claimed them, for a small charge; there is one today just seventy yards from Little John's grave at Hathersage) is named in later stories as George of the Green, and became a well-known local folk-hero in his own right. He takes on other duties in later stories.

This is one of the earliest stories concerning Robin Hood's encounters with a common yeoman, and follows the familiar theme of disguise, confrontation, fight, defeat, acceptance. The story opens with a description of the pinner himself, a merry lad afraid of nought, and not afraid either to enforce his given duty on whoever transgresses it knight, squire or baron. The pinner is sitting by a thorn tree watching a path when Robin, John and Will Scarlet appear. Either wilfully or otherwise, they make their way over to him across a field of ripening corn. The pinner states the obvious; the men have damaged the crops by walking through them, and he asks them to turn around and go back the way they came.

Robin replies that the pinner is a bold man to presume to give orders to three armed men. The pinner then leaps up (in one story he leaps thirty feet!) and the fight begins; the pinner is also armed with a sword, and bests all three outlaws, breaking their swords and bucklers.

Robin finally asks him, John and Will to stop fighting he then proposes that as the pinner is such a good swordsman he give up his trade, come with them and join their band, offering him a new coat twice a year - one green, the other brown.

The pinner is clearly not happy with his working arrangements; he states he must stay until Michaelmas to receive his wages, but he will then go with the outlaws as he cares as much for his employer as his employer does for him. They then eat together of the pinner's food; ale, beef and bread in a curious twist to the theme of the victim being taken to dine with the outlaws.

Notes
George Green in another tale takes on all three simultaneously, and beats them. This goes away from the established theme of single-combat. As previously stated, more stories feature George as the central figure in the tale with no mention of Robin Hood. These echo George giving Robin more kudos, as he accepts Robin as leader although well-known for his duty and strength already.

Robin Hood and the Curtal Friar

Friar Tuck may have been also known as a separate folk-hero figure locally before becoming associated with Robin Hood. He was originally a monk; he was also a figure of fun in the May Games celebrations, taking the part of the fool or jester. He also has connections with folklore through the opening of the story, with romantic allusions to night-time moons at maytime, with girls and young men regretting the passing of the pagan mating season.

The story is indeed a well-known one, second only to that of Little John - but parts of it now are seldom recounted. Nobody ever hears these days of the friar's fierce hunting-dogs. Robin's actions in both stories are those of a recruiting sergeant or perhaps even territorial.

The earliest story - unfortunately with parts missing - has Robin pledging he will eat nor drink until he has seen the cutted friar (possibly another word for curtailed or short-frocked in other words, the friar hitches up his skirts secured by a rope around his waist). The friar is known to be in the vicinity of a nunnery at Fountains Abbey. Robin hides the outlaw band in some bushes, then sets off alone armed with helmet, sword and buckler.

He spots the friar near a river. Robin asks the friar to serve him for Sweet Charity's sake to carry him over the river to save him getting wet. The friar agrees to do so, to do a good deed for the day. He carries Robin Hood across the river, but dumps him off on the opposite bank and draws his sword, he then forces Robin - who he has recognised - to carry him back again. This done, Robin tricks the friar into taking him up again, but this time the friar drops Robin in the water halfway over. A fight ensues, ending with Robin blowing his hunting horn and the outlaws come running. As the friar sees he is outnumbered, he shouts for his dogs - six fearsome beasts who come running up. The friar then prepares to lay them on, but is stopped by Robin who says he would rather fight three fierce dogs than the friar again; this breaks the ice, and they talk. Robin invites the friar into the greenwood.

A later tale in the seventeenth century follows the same theme, but the subject of the friar comes up when Robin is praising John for his hunting skills, saying there is nobody better. Will Scarlet then describes the curtal friar, well-known for a good archer and swordsman. Robin as usual says he will see this friar, and dresses for a battle. The friar is similarly attired when they meet; Robin does not ask the friar courteously to carry him over the water, but rather at threat of his life - in the initial fight, Robin shoots all his arrows at Tuck who manages to deflect them with his small shield. They then set to with swords Robin is forced back, and becoming tired he asks the friar for a favour. He blows his hunting-horn and the outlaws appear. The Friar then asks a favour in return and shouts out his fierce dogs; this time he does lay them on - two dogs rip Robin's coat off his back and his men cannot shoot them with arrows as the dogs catch the shafts in their mouths!

It is Little John who appears and saves the day; he tells the friar who he is, that the man he is fighting is Robin Hood, and to call off his dogs or he will shoot them and then the friar. The friar does not agree to do so until John has shot six of the dogs. The friar now calls a halt - he will agree to end the fighting, and call a truce for discussion. Robin Hood asks the friar to leave his haunts and come with them into the greenwood at Nottingham; he will be paid a fee each Sunday, and at each holiday in the year get a new robe.

The stories significantly do not have the friar agree at its close to join Robin in the greenwood; the earliest closes by saying that for seven years the friar has kept Fountain Dale, not yielding to knight, earl or lord.

Notes
The last verse in the later story names Fountains Dale as the friar's keep or hermitage. What the knight, earl or lord were trying to get the friar to yield to is not made clear; it is possible they too tried their hand in combat with him as he was a well-known swordsman, and left beaten. In a tale about Friar Tuck a hint as to his past is revealed - he was

once a knight himself, but took holy orders (like Brother Cadfael in the popular stories by Ellis Peters).

Fountains Abbey was not a nunnery or a convent, but was actually a Cistercian monastery. There was some animosity between the occupants of Fountains Abbey and those of St Mary's near York because of a past split due to the interpretation of what poor really meant when applied to a monk!

Significantly, no mention is made in the story of the friar's size, ale capacity, or appetite for food. He appears to be an ordinary-looking man on the outside; no mention is made of his name.

Robin Hood and Little John

Probably the best known of all the tales of Robin Hood is his encounter with Little John. The story may post-date the appearance of John in the other tales; but it may have been created later to give more detail about John's origins and put more flesh on his bones as he fast became an important character in the stories. He also gains his great stature from this story, first published around the year 1600.

The story also takes the opportunity to give Robin himself a personal detail, such as his age given as twenty years old. However, this story doesn't state how long Robin has been an outlaw, or what he was outlawed for; the only allusion to outlawry is the fact that their shooting the King's deer is mentioned as commonplace matter-of-fact. It does give an impression that Robin is newly-started on the outlaw trail when he asks John to become his by joining his band and accepting his livery.

The story begins with Robin already an outlaw with a few of his band, telling them he is off to find some sport as there has been no excitement for over a fortnight. He warns his men to stay hidden, but to come to the sound of his hunting-horn should they hear it.

Presently, he comes to a narrow bridge spanning a wide brook; on the other side, he spots a man, in later stories seven feet tall, his limbs were large also preparing to use the bridge. Typically, Robin nocks an arrow to his bow and tells the man to halt. The man, seeing what appears to be a rather cocky youth, says in reply that if Robin touches the bowstring he will thrash him. Robin points out that the man speaks like a fool; he can shoot him before the man could even reach him. Cleverly, the man points out that to threaten a man with an arrow when the man himself has only a staff is nothing to be proud of; indeed the act of a coward! Robin's colour rises at this - he tells the man to stay where he is until he too has armed himself with a staff and then he will fight him, man-to-man.

Robin returns, having cut himself an oak branch, to find the man is waiting, and the fight begins. Robin gets the first blow in; but gets a crack on the head in return, causing blood to appear. He then attacks the man furiously, but cannot break the man's guard, finally the man strikes Robin and knocks him off the bridge and into the brook.

The man good-naturedly shouts down to Robin, floating in the water. Robin concedes defeat, and wades to the bank to pull himself out. He then blows his horn, and the outlaws appear from hiding. One of them - Will Stutely - asks Robin what has happened? Robin tells him, and the band move to throw the man into the brook too - Robin stops them. He tells the band what a stout fellow John is; and then makes an offer to John himself that if he will join them he shall have a sum of money (threescore and ten) and a new lincoln-green coat too. Robin also says he shall be taught to be an archer. They shake hands on it.

The man says his name is John Little; Stutely suggests he should be re-christened as Little John, and offers to be his godfather. The band then go off to feast and drink; the christening takes place, with Stutely and seven men standing in a circle around John. Robin gives John a new coat of green cloth and also a powerful longbow as a gift.

Notes

The impression I got from first reading this story is that Robin has not been outlawed long. He asks John to become his and wear his livery; the temptation is to assume that Robin is out recruiting and initially sought to impress John with the appearance of Might alone. John is obviously a clever chap - he deftly avoids being shot by querying the younger man's courage, getting him to relinquish his bow and fight at a disadvantage. John puts up with Robin's attacks for a while, then becomes angry when the young man persists and grows bad-tempered. The water in the brook cools Robin's temper faster than being thrashed or injured in a fight.

No mention is made of John's destination prior to meeting Robin Hood at the bridge, nor is a reason given for him so quickly joining the outlaw band. The band are obviously so overjoyed to have him they even ask, and the woodland feast seals the business.

Little John can have no doubt what he is getting into; Robin tells him they are poachers already, and fully intend to rob any passing Bishop of his purse in order to provide finance.

It is only in a later tale that gives Little John his great stature and size; prior to that, he appears to be like the curtal friar - just an ordinary chap.

Robin Hood and Alan-a-Dale

A story away from the generally established theme of earlier stories. Robin now shows he has gained some wisdom in his dealings with men, and is becoming a field commander familiar with military-style tactics, quick planning and delegation; he seeks to defeat his chosen adversary in this story by his wits rather than with his steel. He is also seen to do somebody a good turn out of compassion, rather than persistently infuriate the Sheriff's authority alone, or rob the passing clergy of their money.

In the story, Robin has seen a young man dressed in fine scarlet clothes tripping over the countryside, singing a song as he went along. Next day, he spots him again but this time he is not wearing his fine clothes, and appears to be rather crestfallen. John and Much stop him; and bring him before Robin. Robin asks him for money to spare; the young man answers he has five shillings and a gold ring, which he has saved for his wedding for seven years; the wedding was to have been the previous day, but the bride was taken away by her father and promised to another man, an old knight, to be married that day.

Robin asks if the young man will pay him to help him out in this matter? The young man repeats he has no money nor access to any; all he can offer is his loyal service. Robin asks how far it is to the church where the wedding is to be, and Alan tells him it is no more than five miles. Robin sets off to go to the church at once, after giving his orders.

Robin appears at the church, only to be collared by the priest, who demands to know what he is doing there? Robin replies he is the best harper in the county, come to play at the wedding. The bishop is much pleased - he loves music. Robin refuses to play before the arrival of the bride and groom.

The groom now appears, bringing the bride; a good-looking girl dressed in fine clothes. Robin declares it no fit match, and blows his hunting-horn loudly. The outlaws appear from hiding, twenty four archers, looking very threatening, marching in a form of military formation Alan arrives first, and passes Robin his bow and arrows. Robin declares that the wedding will still take place, but between Alan and the girl instead of the old knight. The bishop at once objects, as the banns haven't been read three times as the law decrees; Robin merely pulls of the bishops cloak and mitre and hands them to Little John, who puts them on.

John then asks the congregation seven times if the wedding should go on, rather than just three - obviously nobody objects! Robin gives the bride away himself; afterwards the whole band return to the greenwood.

Notes
Robin significantly does not step out to meet Alan when he first sees him; he just lets him pass by unhindered this may reflect the outlaws growing indentification with robbing only the rich in the form of the high clergy. Even next day, when he sees Alan again - this time very upset - it is John and an outlaw named Midge (probably intended to be Much) who waylay him. Robin has delegated the prior confrontation for the first time in this story.

Where Robin would get a harp from in his haste to prevent the wedding at the church for his disguise as a musician is anyone's guess; he refuses to play for the bishop before he sees the bride and groom as he probably doesn't have one!

Similarly, the rejoinder that the girl should have married the old knight for his money and had Alan on the side is not reflected in her behaviour as she doesn't appear to be accorded any views on the subject.

The story is short and sweet; with a happy ending. What the old knight and the bride's father (who doesn't appear in the story) have to say about it all was not recorded!

Robin obviously enjoys the enmity of the old knight afterwards; perhaps it was he that hired Guy of Gisborne or Red Roger by taking out a contract on Robin Hood in return for this insult? In one more modern story, the old knight character is Guy of Gisborne; Robin also serves Guy a second time by saving Maid Marian from a similar fate! From this point, it is easy to place Guy as someone who wishes to kill Robin Hood.

But - the losers in the stories of Robin Hood get short shrift; nobody cares about what they think!

Robín Hooð anð Maíð Maríaɲ

A rather odd and far-fetched tale where Marian is introduced again after featuring in 1598 in Anthony Mundays famous play *The Downfall and Death of Robert, Earl of Huntington*. She and Robin are forced to part when Robin goes into the greenwood (having been presumably outlawed, although this story still doesn't say anything about the whys or wherefores). Marian is heartbroken; she dresses as a man and goes into the forest fully-armed to look for Robin. He too is out and about fully-armed, and when the two meet for some reason they don't recognise each other and fight for hours wounding each other before Robin asks for the fighting to stop, and his opponent to join the outlaw band. Marian at that point recognises Robin's voice, reveals all and the couple are re-united; much kissing and cuddling follows. Little John arrives at this point and sees what is going on - he takes up his bow and disappears into the forest on a convenient errand - to shoot a deer for the feast to celebrate Marian's arrival; the feasting ends with Robin, Marian and John walking off into the forest. Marian decides to stay in the greenwood and they all live happily ever after.

Notes

Robin and Marian fight for a time and both wound each other before recognising each other - highly unlikely! It highlights the disguise element in other tales by giving one to each main character and if staged as a play must have been great for the audience to watch (girls in plays at the time of the story were played by young boys; but any stage-fight must have been as exciting for them as the 1938 screen encounter with Errol Flynn and Basil Rathbone was for me). John appears as an aside in the story and does not take his usual important role, except to be seen to be intimate with both other main characters. The story sticks to the established central theme of an encounter, fight, then a proposal from Robin to the opponent to join the outlaw band.

Robin Hood - The Noble Fisherman

In this short story, Robin sets off, through boredom, to Scarborough, where he adopts an alias as Simon of the Lee and gets a job on a ship working as a fisherman. Despite feeling both seasick and homesick, Robin spots a French warship coming to attack them; the Master of the vessel loses his bottle and Robin saves the day, shooting several Frenchmen with arrows, and finally boarding the warship and capturing it. He then proposes to give the British crew half the spoils; the Master persuades him to keep the vessel as its owner - the cargo is then found to be twenty thousand pounds in gold bullion! Robin gives half of this to the crew, and intends to use the rest to build a home for the oppressed back on dry land.

Notes

This story is not so well-known as *Robin Hood and the Viking Pirates*, the setting of which is nearby Ravenscar. The author of the story appears to give credence to the story by setting the story near Robin Hood's Bay near Whitby (a town also linked with other Robin Hood stories). Its only redeeming factor for me is the outcome of Robin taking to the water seasick, homesick and named for a landlubber by the Master but ending with Robin as a sea-hero cast in the same mould as King Alfred, Walter Raleigh or Francis Drake. In *Robin Hood and the Viking Pirates*, a far more distant origin can be speculated for the setting of the story; the days of Edward the Confessor - pre-Norman Conquest. Little John appears in this story, but no other outlaws at all appear in *The Noble Fisherman*. Both stories may have been written with an audience of Yorkshire fishermen in mind!

Robin's adopted alias in this tale echoes another tale where he is the husband of Maid Marian, who is the daughter of the impoverished knight Sir Richard of the Lea whom Robin meets in the earlier *Lytell Geste* stories. In this tale, he has children too - the author may have been trying to give Robin a dynasty to promote some future stories, as occurred much later on the big and small screen after Errol Flynn's *Adventures of Robin Hood*!

Footnote

The Rymes of Robin Hood by R B Dobson and J Taylor (Alan Sutton Press) is the best book to acquire in my opinion for a good selection of original ballads and stories; it has an introduction to each one and also appendices of other useful information. An amended and updated version is available. Jim Lees illustrated hardback book is also excellent but impossible to find!

2. There are as many storybooks (in all shapes and sizes) as there are tales; they are far too numerous to list here. The

antique ones I have in my collection here are complete with marvellous illustrations in colour and I'm still finding new ones to add to them each year!

The Man behind the Myth research aspect

Anyone can speculate within the established legend beginning with the ballads about what Robin Hood and his band might have looked like, in any historical period. But to consider what made him tick by looking inside the stories is another matter. Before getting to grips with the individual, let us first try and deal with the outlaws as a group entity.

What first brought them into the public eye?
The early ballads are vague on this; but one later story has him outlawed at an early age due to killing, in self-defence, one of the King's Foresters; another (based on a more modern slant) has him as a young noble outlawed by a cunning plan of the Sheriff to steal his lands out from under him. Whatever put him in the forest drove him for a good many years to actively pursue a policy of revenge tempered with judgement. In any guerrilla war, the hearts and minds of the people must be taken into account; action against them will only serve to isolate you further and remove from use any hope of support and information. Robbing from all and sundry with nought in return places you in the ranks of the many other outlaw bands roving the counties, out for nothing but profit; but nobody remembers them, so we are looking for something extra with Robin Hood.

Most writers concur that in terms of Robin Hood, outside of his particular haunt and out of earshot of the abbots and Sheriff, they heard nothing but good. Certainly anyone feeling his wrath feels it as a result of attempting to kill him or one of his band, or as a result of him temporarily losing his temper due to being bested in one of the stories instances of personal combat. His temper is kept under control for the most part - everyone who beats him on the road or in forest combat then falls a victim to his charm and joins his band of men. This is not the action of a vindictive and bloodthirsty bandit chieftain; more a recruiting sergeant for an army. This echoes that the main grievance - the incentive for becoming an outlaw - is a common one throughout the area.

In the end, it is the Sheriff himself - not without men-at-arms, foresters and also those who have for some reason their own personal scores to settle - that go into Sherwood with the intention to put a stop to him and his band once and for all.

Is Robin Hood the chief of a band of outlaws?
Delegation is the key to command; around him Robin has a group of men who lead smaller groups of men, or go out on their own to seek adventure. We don't, at the beginning, know their stories, but we begin to learn of them later. At the opening of this story, he tells the group what their aims are; not wholesale plunder of the countryside around them, but a planned and concerted attack on selected social and economic targets. Apparently the decision has already been democratically taken that Robin is the leader, and he has the command at that time.

The areas in which they operate are extensive; no means of instant communication are available, and yet he is sending out his men with specific orders - he must trust them out of sight. To do this he must have known them for a long time, and had the opportunity to view their characters. The same works in reverse - they must know him, and trust him.

Once out of sight, they must have some plan to meet up and debrief. An arranged rendezvous has probably been set, on a particular day. The band are apparently self-sufficient, as they are seen to make no preparations regarding food and drink. One of the orders is to seek out and bring back some traveller to dine with them in the forest; this order gainsays that at that selected spot food and drink will already be there. It concludes that other outlaws have already been given orders for the collection and storage of these stores. The simple logistics of maintaining a military force in the field, digging latrines, fetching water, stockpiling rations, laundry, establishing an ammunition supply etc are not those aspects that most readers of adventure stories would find appealing or interesting. These aspects are apparently glossed over and we are left to assume that somebody, somewhere is taking care of it all for the common good of the group. In some stories, outlaws go out and shoot a deer for a spontaneous celebratory feast in the same way as we would pop to the corner shop for a loaf of bread; reducing traditional hunting skills through the storyteller to the same stealth required by anyone to shop at a modern supermarket.

In any emergency, the group must have some selected spot to meet; divided they are useless, united they could stand (even though unlikely against an armed force). This spot must have a small supply depot, for the basic needs of outlaws living on a knife-edge are still the important basics such as food and drink and somewhere safe and relatively comfortable to sleep. Somewhere to recover, re-supply, replenish your stomach, link up with the rest of the group and make a new plan based on the change of circumstances is a bonus.

These spots must have been well-known, easy to find or easily recognisable to the outlaw : we are talking about an area of dense woodland twenty miles deep and six miles wide. Could an emergency have occurred? I think this unlikely; no well-armed force of men-at-arms and archers would be sent into the forest from a medieval strongpoint on a long-term basis to seek out a small band of human pests and hope to exist as an entity long enough to find them in that expanse without prior knowledge from an informer - and with good information you don't then require a large force. Like all terrorists and similar para-military groups, they have - to regular military forces - the infuriating ability to strike anywhere in a large area then simply melt into the surrounding background to strike somewhere else at a later date.

Yet there must have been some form of everyday law and order out on patrol or there would be no need for men outlawed to be forced to live in the forest anyway; equally, by the time an outlaw band have grown and become a real pain and seen to be so by the authorities they are probably well-enough organised to expect and be ready for authority doing just that. For a sensible band of outlaws, a retreat from soldiers trained in warfare - heavy infantry clad in metal armour and supported by artillery - would be quite prudent! As today, troublemakers would lie low until the threat has passed. For the soldiers to find a small camp, a few pots and what food and drink couldn't be picked up and taken away, would not be a great loss to the outlaws. The outlaws, if threatened, could disperse using their greater mobility when the soldiers couldn't, knowing full well that when the soldiers supplies or incentives ran out, they would turn back. If the soldiers did keep coming, the outlaws could temporarily retire into the next shire where a different jurisdiction ruled.

We are now talking tactics and a battle-plan. If a main camp is established, then we need to consider the facility of an alarm to call in our small bands and concentrate to meet the enemy; to defend our stores and base under our commanders personal control. This alarm as we've already seen is not one that could be instantly applied - even the hunting horn we often see has practical limitations; rather an efficient alarm depends on foreknowledge of the enemies' plans and movements... what a modern military mind names intelligence.

What else would the outlaws need?

1. A treasury springs to mind, in which to store the profits from the robberies until they can be distributed; the siting of which is not an easy decision for someone to make in the midst of a gang of thieves who all know the valuables are there; or a Fence to receive the non-spendable booty and distribute it around the country.

2. Women; their wives and families, or at least some form of leavening female presence. Without it, they would be at each other's throats after a time or simply resort to some sort of vice like drugs or alcohol.

3. Metalworkers, bakers, butchers, brewers, tailors and shoemakers - the list is great. These are specialist workers, and don't grow on trees or generally live under them. They all require tools, workshops and materials.

I could go on, but the ones listed so far are all based in the town or village in this era. We can transfer these facilities into the greenwoods, but it takes us back to a point we have already discussed - mobility. Picking up an anvil from a forge or a barrel full of ale is not so easy as hoisting your bag of personal belongings and legging it into the trees in the face of an imminent threat! But would we need to? These are every-day acceptable tradesmen's businesses; the only difficulty we have here is in the forces of law and order connecting them with supplying the needs of outlaws, and removing them.

We are returning to a previous point about the 'something extra' in the legend of Robin Hood; why he is regaled as a folk-hero amongst the common people. The common grievance of the outlaws must have been shared by them too, even though not outlaws. The outlaws many of them former neighbours of these tradesmen - would enjoy the sympathy of many of these folk in any common argument against authority. Many of their family members could still be within acceptable boundaries of society in the same village or town. Some - and it would not require many of them to do so - could secretly support the outlaw band by supplying the requirements in terms of the above needs in return for protein in the form of meat, or cash payments - both in short supply for the common folk in the early medieval era. In the harsh winters of this period, when road traffic was all but ended, the outlaws could move in with them for warmth and support and not have to continue to survive in their rough and ready woodland habitats.

Obviously, we need to consider what the risk to any supporter would be. Who were the authorities that would punish the villagers for doing so? How could they find out that it was going on at all? Were effective forces of law and order ranged against an outlaw? When would they strike? What did they consist of ?

We are moving rapidly away from the ideal of a small band of outlaws living on deer and what they could steal, paying for it when necessary by taking cash by highway robbery from passing travellers, clerics and officials; but approaching a possibility that could have sustained the romantic image of Robin Hood for 800 years. We are now also approaching speculation which can only be partly supported by the existing historical evidence. We have discussed events and possibilities that lean towards a group having both a strong leader, an efficient organisation and a dynamic plan.

What makes up the sort of man who is a leader of outlaws? Traditionally, outlaws (and their bed-fellows, pirates and bandits) are avaricious but colourful men of fortune who take what they like when they like for profit, then blend back into the vast and often harsh backdrop forest, desert or ocean - to strike again at another point. They live life on a razor-edge, with the ever-present threat of capture by the authorities, a fair trial and the subsequent ugly punishment. They apparently live when not working a life of carefree fun, drinking alcohol only to excess, eating copious quantities or roast meat when they are hungry or sober, but are extremely professional in what they do; and are at war with everybody.

A pirate - in popular belief - is also seen to run the risk of falling foul of their shipmates; being marooned or made to walk the plank, being thrown to the sharks or simply sliced up by an aggressive fellow seaman.

A bandit lives around an open fire in a mountain cave or at a remote desert oasis, drinking and waiting for the next poor traveller to come within reach. Both have manly - but often crude and cruel - pastimes for their leisure hours to allay the boredom, or sprawl in slumber after a night of excesses. Women - when seen - are there for one purpose only.

The picture we have is of a potentially explosive lethal mixture of bloodthirsty homicidal maniacs grouped together in circumstances they can't get away from who are liberally festooned with edged weapons or firearms and who are bent on grabbing as much as they can from each other, unless some outside influence in the form of a threat or easy pickings brings them to their senses. Traditionally, the only thing stopping the group or crew from becoming a whirlwind of mutual and sanguinary disaster is a strong leader.

I use the word strong; but not just in a physical sense. He must have a powerful will, too. To exercise control over a group as we have just outlined calls for qualities far above the usual sort found in everyday groups of men. These are not disciplined soldiers, so obedience to rank would not apply; they have no civilised creed or code, so considerations of good manners and fair play can be ruled out - although in certain historical circumstances for some groups we can argue for a religious bonding. The only thing worshipped here is precious stones or metals; it is not a democracy allegiance is given to the one who provides the latter; failure to do so means a quick end, and a new leader.

Robin Hood shares some of these qualities, not all. The hard-hitting, big-drinking, roast meat-eating, carefree physical fun and a degree of the manly sports aspects still hold true. But gone is the avarice, the gratuitous violence, the self-centred greed and the obedience to orders only when it suits these are replaced by sharing, loyalty, samaritanism and democracy.

What makes our band of outlaws different; what stopped them starting out - or degenerating like every other - into a band of cut-throats? Could it be about the leadership qualities of Robin Hood; but where are any other examples in historical or present-day reality?

One of the traditional explanations thrown in to explain why men can turn at the drop of a hat into rabid beasts who prey on their fellows is that circumstances made them so. In the case of romantic pirates and bandits, it is often identified (especially in cinema) that the authorities are worse than they are - cruel, unjust and uncaring. They are forced by these circumstances to the life they now lead; the unspoken ideal is that it is unnatural for men to be this way , that they could choose it out of their own free will and enjoy it is out of the question. They remain so only as they now have no choice; underneath their carefree happy life they are portrayed as deeply sad or troubled men in rare moments of contemplation. They have a happy life; but invariably a short one and they make the most of it too as they can invariably see this short and sticky end looming over the horizon in the form of a rope, cannonball or bullet.

Robin Hood's activities in the greenwoods in the stories went on for over thirty-five years! *4

For footnotes on the ballads see Conclusion on page 184.

Part Five

Daylight

To officialdom, Robin Hood is still and will remain forever, a criminal. Throughout the fifteenth century, various reported affrays by gangs of young men on a spree as referred to as emulating Robin Hood and his Merry Men, seen undoubtably as a threat to law and order and the peace. He is used here as a role model for gangs of young men; dressing as Robin Hood and the Merry Men during the May Day Festivals was acceptable, even to the church (officials dressed in costumes - sometimes paid for by and stored in the church - as Robin and his Men collected money from the crowd at these festivals for Poor Relief, sometimes with a bit of play-acting thrown in as symbolic of the past highway robbery of Robin for the same purpose). What wasn't acceptable for the organisers were gangs of young rowdies emulating the other traditions by creating disorder at the festivities afterwards by not doing as they were told, and drinking too much ale.

Robin Hood and Maid Marian played large parts in these May Festivals from the early fourteenth century onwards. Robin was often cast as Lord of Misrule or Disobedience in these festivals, with Marian as his Queen. They were on the whole splendid entertainments with playacting, music and dance and very much looked forward to by the locals. The places where they were celebrated and the actors who played in them became very well-known too; many of the place-names attributed to Robin Hood may be the sites or dwelling-places of actors chosen for these May Games.

In 1598 (by which time many more people are able to read) a play written by a popular playwright Anthony Munday was performed in which Robin is now in reality a nobleman, the Earl of Huntingdon. This may have been done to appeal to the higher classes, as a stout yeoman from the lower orders taking on and defeating the forces of law in the shape of the Sheriff of Nottingham may not have been palatable. He is not fighting against the law, but graft and corruption disguised as the law. He is still loyal to the land (in the form of the King), and is very religious, devoted to the Virgin Mary. Even after Malory's *Morte d'Arthur*, Robin Hood was still the only untainted hero available common folk could identify with.

In 1632, *The True Tale of Robin Hood* by Martin Parker followed on; in 1746 Dr William Stukeley, Fellow of the Royal Society, eminent doctor and country parson, gave the Earl of Huntingdon a family tree taking him back beyond the *Domesday Book*. By 1786 a grave complete with epitaph to Robin Hood at Kirklees was in Richard Gough's illustrated book *Sepulchral Monuments of Great Britain*. By 1795, John Ritson in his *Life of Robin Hood* has chronicled the life and times of Robin by compiling all the available material so far; unfortunately he also chronicled and repeated all the suggestions, suppositions and errors in identification of all his predecessors, in some cases oddly contradicting himself in the same paragraph. Ritson in his introduction states that although Robin is a romantic figure with wide appeal, no definitive evidence existed to place him in any historical reality; Ritson then went on in his book to try and do it.

In 1852, Joseph Hunter tried to re-establish the facts. Hunter was a trained scholar, antiquarian and a local historian. In his work from 1833 until 1861, when he died still serving as Assistant Keeper to the Public Records Office, he edited and published many of the records of medieval government. Hunter was a Yorkshireman, and knew all about the folk tales of Robin Hood. He tried to re-evaluate all the evidence, beginning with the ballads. He found traces of actual history that closely matched the ballads - the travels of Edward our comely King in the ballad, matched only the passage of Edward II in 1323; in 1324 a Robert Hood was in the King's service as a servant; this same Robert Hood was entered on the rolls of Wakefield in 1317 and outlawed after his part in the rebellion of the Earl of Lancaster and his subsequent defeat by Edward II at Boroughbridge in 1322. A nest of outlaws and rogues existed in Barnsdale (named in the ballads, and only ten miles from Wakefield) and it was suggested that it was there that Robert Hood fled and sought refuge in 1322; becoming reconciled with the King in 1324 and taking up service with him. Shortly after that, his name disappears from the royal rolls and it is said he returned to Barnsdale and his outdoor life. Hunter didn't find any firm link between the Robert Hood of Wakefield and Robert Hood the King's Porter; but he did find out many errors by past researchers into Robin Hood. He did enjoy a bit of lively speculation as part of his presentation but it had an unfortunate result. In time the errors he uncovered were disregarded, and his speculation accepted as simple truth by other writers who came later.

Sir Walter Scott had made Robin a rebel, standing for Saxons against Norman oppression in the novel *Ivanhoe* in 1820; his novel reached an enormous audience. Many other writers and poets wrote about Robin Hood too, changing him over and over through adaptations to suit their understandings. In 1840 Pierce Egan wrote *Robin Hood and Little John*, a story especially for children. Tennyson in a poem gave Maid Marian a new father; the poor knight who Robin aids in one of the ballad stories. Each tag onto Robin the best of the historical attributes, and a few of their own too. In 1952 the Robert Hood of Wakefield unearthed by Joseph Hunter was being promoted in a new book as the real man behind the legend by another Yorkshire historian, James Walker.

By 1960, many of Hunter's ideas and those of others taking Robin Hood up into Yorkshire fell on deaf ears. Robin Hood had firmly established himself without any help from any historians (indeed despite them) in the place where he was to be worshipped as a folk-hero beyond any other - Sherwood Forest. The two names were now inextricably joined. They would be welded together in the next phase of Robin Hood's existence which brought together both the oral story-telling and May Day traditions and ballads as never before, to a vast audience . using cinema and television.

Part Six

Suppertime

"Second star on the right; straight on till morning"
Captain James Tiberius Kirk, part of another legend
(With apologies to J M Barrie)

As a small child, I can well remember being taken from our summer camp in Clumber Park with my fellow Cubs and Brownies across the county border into Sherwood Forest to see the enormous Major Oak under which Robin Hood, Little John, Maid Marian, Friar Tuck, Will Scarlett and the rest of the Merry Men had sat many an evening around the campfire, eating roast venison and drinking ale. In nearby Nottingham Castle, the Sheriff sat alone in an upstairs room frowning with clenched fists because once again as ever he had been outsmarted by Robin Hood.

As we left skipping up the path, the greenwoods echoed to our falsetto voices, singing *"Robin Hood, Robin Hood, riding thru the glen. Robin Hood, Robin Hood, with his band of men . Robbed from the Rich, gave to the Poor. Robin Hood, Robin Hood, Robin Hood, Robin Hood"*. Many of us were looking into the dark glades of the forest, hoping and fully expecting an outlaw with a cheeky grin and twinkling eyes to appear clutching his bow and arrow. That one didn't appear did not dampen our enthusiasm. At camp next day we were all outlaws, clutching our home-made bows and arrows from materials purchased at a nearby hardware store, or improvised from the nearby bushes should a persistent lack of pocket money (in my case, always) not provided the wherewithal. We had been to Major Oak, the altar of Robin Hood and sworn the oath of allegiance. His creed was simple; be honest and truthful, enjoy life, be charitable and protect others weaker than you, work hard, stand up for yourself and do not fear the outdoor life. Many of us were Wolf Cubs at the time and later became Boy Scouts, and we all identified with Robin Hood a great deal (as any of you that were or are boy scouts or girl guides will still understand). Ah, things were different then!

As we were safely tucked up in bed, after devouring our suppers of roast venison and ale (in reality, biscuits and cocoa) in our dreams Robin Hood sat basking in the firelight under his tree, surrounded by his merry men, all smiling and safe in the knowledge that they were safely cherished in the hearts and minds of the English people.

And not just them; I was reminded of this event in 1994 when I was deep in Russia, when some chance local acquaintance asked me where I came from.

"England.." I replied, *"..Nottingham"*.

"Ah!" he exclaimed, *"Robin Hood!"*

I later found he only knew about twenty words in English.

One mile from where I was born lies Loxley. Again as a boy I recall being shown by someone at nearby Loxley Firth a tumbled-down ancient ruin in the shape of a pile of stones in a ditch and being told it was the remains of the cottage where Robin Hood was born (I didn't believe the tale, but the piece of stone I picked up as a souvenir from the pile then is still in my possession even after all these years). A nearby hostelry The Robin Hood was said to be one of his drinking haunts, when not away robbing the Rich; another local landmark just passing from memory then was nearby Robin Hood's Bower. A natural fault in the gritstone cliffs at Stanage Edge at the edge of the moors to the west of Sheffield where I used to sit and eat my morning snack on several hikes bears the name Robin Hood's Cave. Two miles further west lies Hathersage; in the churchyard there lies the grave of Little John, and a nearby hollow in a field is declared the former site of the cottage where he was both born and returned to die. Not far from Little John's grave lies Robin Hood's Stoop, where he and Little John once stood and shot an arrow over a mile landing in the churchyard there (where the grave of little John lies today). Close by, near Birchover (an ancient prehistoric site) stands Mock Beggars Castle which is now known as Robin Hood's Stride, an outcrop of rocks overlooking The Nine Maidens stone circle; at its base lies a cave which served in the medieval period as a hermitage, with a large carved cross set in the stone [*1]. This site is documented in ancient times, and a local legend states Robin Hood once stood atop it with one foot on each outcrop, urinating, nine maidens who saw him were so shocked they became petrified!

This is so unlike the behaviour of our Robin we immediately think it linked with some other fellow with a similar name. A prehistoric earthwork near Matlock bears the name Hob's House, after another local folktale. Hob in legend can be at the same time as big as a house, or as small as a mouse. Perhaps this gives us a clue as to the origin of the former legend. Within ten miles of Hob's House there are over twenty well-known landmarks which bear the connection of Robin Hood; his stone, well, gate, close, etc. At Chatsworth House, a deep gorge is known as Robin Hood's Leap ; it is said he was so overjoyed to see Maid Marian after a long time away he leapt it in order to reach her the sooner! Mr Jim Lees points out that in two historical displays one at Fountain Dale House, the other at Thoresby Hall where two modern longbows were included, they assumed the names Friar Tuck's Bow and Maid Marian's Bow just by association within a short passage of time even though no claim was made as such by the items themselves !

The local Derbyshire custom of Well-Dressing still has strong pagan undertones, and they were also the sites of May Festivals. The South and East Yorkshire claims in connection with Robin Hood established originally in the ballads by the place-names used - raises its head every so often, causes a flurry of argument with Old Nottingtonians as to county ownership, then dies down once again for another year (recently historians from Lincolnshire, Staffordshire, Shropshire, Rutland and Derbyshire have also thrown their hats in the ring for possession of the outlaws heritage, valued by different persons for various reasons).

Some authors have sat in judgement on Robin Hood like the Sheriff of Nottingham on a prisoner, putting him on trial under the microscope and stripping away each veneer carefully applied each century until bare bones are revealed which in most cases have mouldered to dust. For each of the serious studies, there are ten to fifteen light-hearted ones circulating in print each year with glorious illustrations accompanying the stories, and suit the eye and pocket of children and adult alike.

Robin Hood stories and songs circulated, expanded and grew throughout the sixteenth and seventeenth centuries. From 1700, and by the middle of the eighteenth century he was firmly rooted in and around Nottingham, the largest town in the area claiming him for ownership. In the later and more prolific ballads, plays and songs - designed for a larger and wider audience, Nottingham clearly had the enormous tavern and theatre capacity to benefit from them. Other sites at the time as possibly described in the original material Barnsdale, for instance, near Wakefield - were rural backwaters far removed from the large populations of the big towns. Nottingham was a large and important town throughout medieval history and beyond and did figure in the original material; the Sheriff of Nottingham and Sherwood Forest were seen to be Robin Hood's chief antagonist and main theatre of operations.

A whole host of B-movies featuring Robin Hood in a variety of locations outside Sherwood and up against everything from cattle rustlers to pirates on the high sea were turned out from 1920 onwards; with the exception of the magnificent Douglas Fairbanks, many are not worth watching (in my humble opinion). For my generation, Richard Greene, the actor playing the outlaw on television and in cinema during the sixties was Robin Hood.

For the previous generation, it was of course this time in sound and colour - the equally magnificent Errol Flynn in the 1938 classic *The Adventures of Robin Hood* with Olivia de Havilland as a doe-eyed superlative Maid Marian (there were other Robins of course, the most notable follow-on Robin Hoods behind Errol Flynn and Richard Green being Richard Todd and John Derek). Sean Connery played an older and wiser Robin Hood in *Robin and Marian* who still managed to beat the Sheriff of Nottingham albeit very narrowly and being mortally wounded in doing so. This was later followed by a very successful television series *Robin of Sherwood*, with actors Michael Praed and Jason Connery taking the lead. The popularity of the series was said to be due to its association in many of the story-lines with the mystical aspects of earlier legends.

Walt Disney made *Robin Hood*, a full-length feature-film cartoon at the same time, with animal characters : King Richard and Prince John both lions, and Robin and Marian both artful foxes. Little John was the lumbering bear, straight out of Disney's *Jungle Book*.

Two big budget feature films of the nineties, for the UK *Robin Hood* with Patrick Bergin and for the USA *Robin Hood; Prince of Thieves* with Kevin Costner (which eclipsed the latter made at the same time, although many Robin-ites here say it was the better of the two films) both giving the legend a fresh slant on familiar themes. From then on, anything is possible for Robin Hood. *Rocket Robin Hood*, a short-lived television cartoon adventure in which Robin had a jet propelled backpack, had Sherwood Forest on a moon and Robin operating in outer space - Darth Vader would have made an excellent Sheriff of Nottingham; I leave the obvious comparison for Luke Skywalker to the reader! *The New Adventures of Robin Hood* which began on UK Channel Five Television in July 1998 follows the traditions established by the now cult-status television serials *Hercules* and *Xena, Warrior Princess*. In two of the pilot episodes, Robin Hood encounters both Viking raiders landing in their longships and a Mongol horde rampaging through Sherwood Forest! They will both no doubt eventually get booted out of England at the hands - and feet - of Robin's boys and girls.

Thirty-five years to the day after I first stood under the Major Oak in Sherwood as a little boy at the beginning of this section, I met Robin Hood there as the sun went down, longbow in hand, surrounded by his band. It was Midsummer's Night, the Solstice the beginning of the end, before the circle turns again and the Dance starts over once more. I lit the solstice flame on that occasion with fire and water (the flint and steel in my tinderbox) and then wind and earth combining the four elements to make fire in the spirit of the occasion.

In one of the stories Robin Hood dies, after leaving his favourite stamping-ground and being betrayed as foretold in omen - by a woman; a common form of folk hero demise. Instead of making an end, it just marked the end of the beginning.

Footnote
1. Due to vandalism in the seventies, this cave and those of Robin Hood at Cresswell Crags are now no longer open for access without special permission.

Part Seven

Evening

The Green Man and the Lord of the Hunt had a little friend, Robin Goodfellow. In Shakespeare's *Midsummer Nights Dream*, Oberon the King of the Faeries is aided and abetted by Puck in his dealings with Titania, Queen of the Faeries. The Norse Gods endured Loki, also a mischievous prankster.

There are many other comparisons; it may well be that all folk tales have but one origin from which they sprouted branches. In our country, there are tales which originate in great antiquity, Celtic then Roman, mingled with Scandinavian and European stories in the mingling of the different peoples coming here and settling. A story in one county of England seems similar to that in another county many miles away, the changes are reflected in the different people who settled in that area long ago.

Folk heroes generally have their companion to sound off against or rescue them from evil doings; a sort of guilty conscience. Robin Hood had Little John; he then gained Maid Marian, Friar Tuck, Will Scarlet, Alan-a-Dale and a whole entourage of others; at one point in the stories over a hundred and fifty men, a sizeable force. As any movie or TV drama writer will tell you, it is always handy for our hero to have companions; they can be used to support him, expand the stories, provide new and fresh adventures; or simply be someone to speak to, rescue or get angry about when they are killed, giving justification to our hero who then goes off and reduces the opposition in a manly and sanguinary form. With a hundred and fifty men, you even storm castles and shake the foundations of Kingdoms. Being surrounded by others also makes our hero more human; less solitary, more gregarious. He can show his feelings, debate important matters, enjoy their company and loyalty, and also establish a dynasty. The fact that so many are there and following him shows him to be above the average sort of chap; managing a band of outlaws that strong in numbers and setting rules and a code of conduct for them must have called for an extraordinary man, and the fact he is there fulfiling that role is seen to be a qualification for admiration toward him on our part.

Who were the other characters in the Robin Hood legend ?

Little John

Little John is unique amongst the Merry Men; he is there with Robin from the start of the ballads in Sherwood and also goes on for a while after his death. He too appears from nowhere, although in the ballads he knows Sherwood very well. He gets two of the ballads to himself; growing from an outlawed good yeoman to a larger-than-life figure seven feet tall with limbs like tree trunks. He is always in Robin's shadow; indeed he is Robin's shadow, strange for such a big man. He is by no means less cunning than Robin; he is also shown to be his equal if not his better at Arms. From the sixteenth century onwards he grows in stature. Old Irish folktales have him in Dublin after Robin's death, shooting

An old tombslab in Hathersage attributed to 'Little John' as the initials 'L' and 'J' are carved upon it. The carving is said to have been done later than the slab was made (the 'J' actually looks like an 'I' due to the period spelling

arrows great distances. On one hill he was supposed to have been caught and hanged; another later tale says not, and he fled to Scotland, to a place named Pettin in Moray Firth where a large man was buried according to three contemporary chroniclers writing around 1500 to 1596. The man was named in the Scots chronicles Little John.

The traditional grave of Little John in Hathersage was opened in 1784, under the supervision of a Captain William Shuttleworth; two long pieces of a thigh bone were found at a depth of six feet. When placed together, the piece measured such a length that it was calculated that the owner would have been ten feet tall (the record for the height of a man in England is William Bradley who stood seven feet nine inches in 1815; the thigh bones were apparently two bones saw-cut to fit together, and possibly not altogether human). Little John's longbow and cap were said to hang in the church; a six and a half foot weapon was inside Cannon Hall near Barnsley in my lifetime. It was attributed to the Eyre family who served as Gentlemen Foresters at some time in the past; their memorial is also in Hathersage church. The old cottage where Little John was said to have spent his final years after Robin's death, destroyed by a fire in the late 19th century, stood to the east of the church; all that remains of it now is a hollow in the ground.

We move to Mansfield, where another cottage said to have been the home of one George Naylor and his son John, both nail-makers by trade, once stood. Close by is the lane over a stream where it is said that he met an old acquaintance (possibly from his army days see later) who cheekily still gave him orders and disputed the passage across the narrow footbridge there, the argument being settled by blows from quarterstaffs in which Robin Hood ended up taking an early bath! From that born-again baptism and rebirth, the true friendship began between Little John and Robin Hood. Little John is a fearsome warrior; his exploits with bow and sword

The traditional grave of Little John at Hathersage

HERE LIES BURIED

LITTLE JOHN
THE FRIEND & LIEUTENANT OF
ROBIN HOOD

HE DIED IN A COTTAGE (NOW DESTROYED)
TO THE EAST OF THE CHURCHYARD
THE GRAVE IS MARKED BY
THIS OLD HEADSTONE & FOOTSTONE
AND IS UNDERNEATH THIS OLD YEW TREE

Close-up of the headstone of the Little John grave

are well depicted in the ballads. In one of them, he draws his sword and with a single blow slices off the head of a monk who has betrayed Robin Hood and is carrying a message about his capture to London; Much is there too, and settles for the monk's terrified servant in the same fashion. Neither seems to break sweat in this; or worry overmuch about murder, leaving the two headless corpses lying in the undergrowth. The upshot is as we are left to suppose is that 'If you ain't with us, you're agin us !' and the end justifies the means.

The Sheriff's chef in Nottingham Castle in another ballad makes a more able opponent for John's sword-swinging, after the Sheriff himself had employed John under the false name of Reynolde Greneleaf - after being impressed with his splendid marksmanship in an archery contest. After Robin has killed Guy of Gisburn, John with unerring marksmanship again - sends an arrow into the fleeing Sheriff of Nottingham. John must have been both a good-looking, physically very fit and charming fellow to boot to get away with all this; he also served as squire to Sir Richard of the Lea on his travels, and on the whole he gives Robin himself excellent competition regarding personal adventures and exploits !

I am indebted to my sister-in-law Shona - a fount of historical knowledge - who points out that compared with the average height of men in England at this time due to diet, disease and hard physical work (average male height under five feet six inches) a mere stripling of only six feet would have been looked on as a giant! Little John's legendary strength possibly came from his past employment as firstly apprentice to, then becoming a blacksmith himself.

Friar Tuck

Friar Tuck was known as early as 1429 as Frere Tucke (Brother Tuck) as a cover-name for a criminal, Richard Stafford of Sussex. By 1475 he has a place in the ballads attached to the May Games portrayed as a trickster and a knave (it is only one letter from Tuck to Puck). He beats Robin at fighting and even lifts his purse; thereby robbing the chief robber, Robin does not have very pleasant things to say about him afterwards. In the play, he takes nothing seriously and is accused by the narrator of just messing about, in other words, he is playing it just for laughs. In the play, Tuck falls into the category of Jester or the Fool. In others, he takes the part of the Abbot of Misrule who succeeds the Lord of Misrule and supervises the celebrations of Christmas. A comparison with Tuck the ale drinking gourmand - to the old Roman god of Bacchus is inevitable. Tuck is anything but pious; friars were austere, pacifist and often hermits - he carries a sword, buckler and staff and doesn't shy away from either a fight where his honour is concerned - or from any later accusations of the then unfashionable Popery; or from any ale-house where his sharp eyes spot a friend imbibing.

Tuck may have been a runaway from the Franciscan abbey nestling under the Castle rock at Nottingham; according to one ballad, he may have been a knight prior to that, as he was noted for his exceptional skill at arms. He certainly enjoyed the outdoor life and hunting. He was a good archer, and kept several hounds for the chase. The name curtal friar comes from the monks trait of often tying up their long habits with a cord at the waist to prevent them dragging on the ground and ease movement; hence curtailing it. Another medieval period name for the cord used for this purpose is a tuck; a name very familiar to modern dressmakers and tailors.

By 1663 the disputed river-crossing where Tuck and Robin in a battle of wits take turns carrying each other over the waters

The Friar Tuck hermitage near Fountain Dale

The place where Friar Tuck and Robin carried each other on their backs through the water

and the subsequent fight takes place at Fountain Dale in Sherwood Forest and centres around the nearby hermitage, sanctuary and holy well where the little stream the Rain once ran, now gone. Tuck resides here in disillusioned solitude after retiring from the world of men. He is persuaded, as are most good folk in the tales after meeting Robin, to join him.

Maîð Maʀîan

Maid Marian is harder to pin down. Robin Hood in the early ballads is shown to be devout and courteous to women of all ages. He regularly attends Mass; indeed he gets into trouble for doing so, as on one occasion he is recognised and men sent to take him, but despite warnings from his band, he won't leave the mass; on another, he is actually caught and arrested by the Sheriff's men. No woman who catches the eye of Robin Hood stands in any danger; she would be sure of an honest courtship from a faithful suitor.

In fact, Robin's devotions are solely to the Virgin Mary; Marian only enters the lists in the May Games in 1508, where she is first partnered with Robin. The word May as used in the festivals is an ancient one, deriving from the anglo-saxon May, Maiden, Maid, Virgin. The oldest English term for the Virgin Mary is Marian. In one medieval story, she is directly linked to an old Celtic goddess Ceridwen, as being the keeper of her magic cauldron of healing, inspiration and rebirth; then Christianised as the communion cup or grail. There are also pointers in the traditional plays to fertility - the maypole itself - and the worship of one of the ancient aspects of the Triple-Goddess of the Moon; named by the Romans and Greeks as Diana or Artemis, who hunts with bow and arrow in the forest. Robin Hood is devoted to all facets of them; it is through Her that he gains strength in the greenwoods; She also lays her protective hand on him whenever outside them. She is also linked in old English folklore with being the mother of the Archer of Love, who the ancients knew of and named Cupid a little boy who never grows up, and who uses a bow to shoot arrows of love !

In the plays written for the May Games, there are references to our maid Marian, the maid Marian and my maid Marion but none to a specific Maid Marian herself. In the Games, she is the Queen of the May, and almost always played by a boy. Samuel Johnson in 1760 refers to a Morris dance in which ten men dance beside the Maid Marian. She is always dressed as a lady, in some instances crowned, and never disports herself at all in the early plays. Only in the later ones beginning in the sixteenth century (possibly due to the growing Puritan influence on seeing what was to them, a pagan ritual) does she begin to become less chaste, and even become referred to as a loose woman. By 1700, through the respect for well-bred ladies after the Restoration of Charles II she becomes once again the demure and virginal young girl of noble birth who is close to the king, who Robin Hood falls in love with at first sight.

By 1800, she is firmly placed at Robin's side as his sweetheart, who in legend joins with her and marries her in Maytime / Beltane under the greenwood tree, in true pagan form - with Friar Tuck joining them - and once again in holy church in nearby Edwinstowe, to satisfy and bring together both the old and new religions.

Maid Marian assumes in the legend the name Fitzwalter. Her tomb is reputedly the one in Little Dunmow Church in Essex; although in reality she probably never existed in a single identifiable mortal form.

The term Merrie-England comes from the country most associated in the medieval era with Mary-Worship.

*Will Scarlet's traditional tombstone under the yew trees;
actually part of the old church tower. Will is reputedly buried
against the old church wall here in an unmarked grave after
being killed in action by one of the Sheriff's men*

Will Scarlett and Alan-a-Dale

Will Scarlet, Scarlock, Scathelocke or Gamwell appears in the stories, sometimes related to Robin Hood being his nephew, born to Robin's sister then living in Mansfield. His ancestry is almost as complicated as his uncle. He lies in legend today under the apex stone of the old church at Blidworth; within view of both Little John's and Tuck's traditional homes. Will is in some of the stories killed by one of the Sheriff's men as part of the tale of Robin's fight with Gisborne; he is immediately avenged by Little John, who then kills the perpetrator.

The role of Alan-a-Dale, the minstrel who joins the band, is sometimes mingled with Will Scarlet in some stories. It is possible that in some May Festival plays, the part of Alan-a-Dale was taken by the singer or storyteller himself; so he could then say, as I once saw done myself, that he knows the story to be true as he himself was There when it happened.

Alan-a-Dale stays loyally with Robin after Robin prevents Alan's girlfriend being married off to an old knight by her father, traditionally at Papplewick church or the older one at Steetley.

Minstrels such as Alan did dress in gaudy and bright colours in fashion as part of their trade (they still do !). The scarlet, the colour associated with his flamboyant dress, was adopted after the Restoration by the British Army as it was the brightest, bravest and boldest colour to be seen in. Was Scathe-locke as proscribed by earlier writers, simply a red-haired man as the name suggests?

Whatever the reason, it was certainly convenient for future minstrels that Robin had such devoted characters near at hand, so well qualified and able to chronicle his adventures in detail and put them to music for posterity in the form of the later generations of audiences.

The author as a merry man circa 1200AD with an English early medieval longbow from ash, by Mr Don Adams; with traditional arrows and associated impedimenta made by the author.

Ye Merry Men

The term merry men may come in association from the old Norman French words *meine* or *mesnie*, meaning 'retinue', taken here to mean a devoutly religious following (see Maid Marian) or household. Will Stutely, David of Doncaster, Much the Miller's Son, George O the Green, Arthur Bland, Gilbert of the White Hand, the Tinker and the Tanner are all men from the lower orders, but all of good yeoman stock. They exist as tradesmen, or by taking venison from the forest and collecting other foodstuffs from the nearby folk who support them in return for services. Some simply serve as eyes or spies. In winter, they would have been exceedingly cold and hungry staying in the forest; the fact is, they weren't in the forest in wintertime - they moved in with the local folk, some of whom were their families anyway, as seen in Scarlet's example. Robin Hood of Sherwood probably had several supporters or maintainers during winter or hard times, from the Abbot of Whitby to the old knight Sir Richard of the Lea; who in one story shelters the outlaws from a full-blown siege, defying the Sheriff of Nottingham pounding on his front door and demanding Sir Richard surrender up the outlaws.

Ye Sheriff of Nottingham

Next to Robin Hood and Little John, the Sheriff is the most prominent character in the legend. He pops up quite early on in the ballad stories, as a cruel tyrant who is seen to be enforcing the King's Will and the Law but for his own purposes; and only when it suits him. Unfortunately, the title Sheriff of Nottingham wasn't created until 1449, by which time our Robin Hood ballad stories are already prevalent throughout England. The forces against which Robin contended would have been in the form and title of either The High Sheriff of Nottingham and Derbyshire; the Constable of Nottingham Castle; or the Chief Justices of the Royal Forests.

The Sheriff of Nottingham on a caparisoned horse, presiding over a recent bit of dirty dealing in the forest.

All these had jurisdiction over offences committed in the area. It would have been one of them who were cast as Robin's arch-enemy.

It was common knowledge that Sheriffs were feathering their own nests; it was common for men to purchase their appointments, and then recoup the cost by making a profit from their duties. In 1170, all the Sheriff's posts in England were suspended by Henry II, pending an inquiry into these practices.

John de Oxenford was a corrupt and very unpopular Sheriff of Nottingham and Derby in 1334-9; so was his predecessor Sir Robert Ingram in 1328-33 who actually helped robbers and rogues active in his area! The infamous Coterel Brothers gang robbed churches, homes and parks; murdered at least four noblemen, and ran a protection racket in Derbyshire and Staffordshire for four years, from 1328 until 1331. Ingram received a share of the profits for turning a blind eye to some of their activities.

Still later John, Baron de Segrave was also very unpopular in his post as Constable of Nottingham Castle and Forest Justice. There were many earlier men too, who lived and served in these posts in the 13th Century, and would have been responsible for curbing and arresting such men as Robin Hood. Documentation of them all exists, some of them were more active than others in their duties. One of them in this period Eustace of Loudham was Sheriff of Yorkshire in 1225-6, and Sheriff of Nottingham and Derbyshire and Forest Justice at the same time, in 1232-3. Catching one Robert Hode being outlawed there in 1226 and imposing the penalties on him would have been one of his duties. Did Eustace first chase Robin Hood in East Yorkshire, then pursue him again in North Nottinghamshire five years later on?

In the stories, it is the Sheriff in the form of the tyrannical civil and forest laws and the thieving clerics lining their own pockets instead of adhering to their vows of poverty and administering to their flocks who are seen as Robin Hood's enemies; the Sheriff grows from a distant figure of authority into a major threat as Robins insults and predations on him grow it, ends with a furious Sheriff attacking the outlaws with all the force he can muster in a spirit of revenge rather than to apply the rule of law. Guy of Gisborne is out in the forest trying to take Robin Hood dead or alive at the same time; again out of revenge or perhaps as an employed mercenary. He has his own mission, it works as Robin Hood is also out looking for Guy, having seen him in a dream the night before. The two meet; Guy is killed. Robin takes on himself the disguise Guy has been using, in order to deceive the Sheriff whose men have killed Will Scarlett and captured Little John. He successfully rescues John who then kills or badly wounds the Sheriff as he attempts to escape.

The Sheriff is always either embarrassed or killed in his clashes with the outlaws; a simple happy ending to every tale every time.

Part Eight

Sweet Dreams

"You can't see the Wood, as there are too many trees there
today."
A fellow tour guide, in 1996

So who was Robin Hood? The simple answer is we'll never
know; because that was what was intended right from the
start. There is enough evidence to suggest two theories as a
basis for the legend as we've explored it. By 1377, in Piers
Plowman there are popular rhymes of Robin Hood cited by the
author, and his name known nationwide - so we could start
there. Before then, we'll look at the historical periods that
Robin Hood was born out of. It makes grim reading ..

There were many periods of social and political unrest in
England in the days of Robin Hood. After the Norman
Conquest, as we've seen there was a period of guerrilla
fighting by the English against the Norman occupation. After
1066 William the Conqueror sent clerks to all parts of his new
kingdom to record every single item of land and property,
down to the last pig and farm implement. The collated
information was written down in two enormous volumes and
used to calculate rates of taxation the *Domesday Book*.

William died on campaign back in Normandy from injuries sustained when he fell from his horse in 1087. The kingdom was split into two England went to one son, William; and Normandy went to another son, Robert. William II of England managed to acquire Normandy too in 1096 when his brother sold it to him for a large sum before his departure for the First Crusade. William put down the ensuing revolts in Normandy from barons thinking they were now independent from his new fealty, then returned to England. Whilst hunting deer in the New Forest, an arrow came from nowhere and struck him in the breast, killing him. Robert was still far away, returning from the Crusade; William's younger brother was on the same hunting trip, he rode straight to London and was crowned, Henry I.

Henry I had a breathing space in which to gain control of England. He first said he would stop the unjust practices of his elder brother; he married a Scots princess to form an alliance with the north, secured the services of the clergy, and then met France and Belgium to secure a buffer zone from the expected invasion when Robert eventually returned home and tried to claim the throne (Robert did try in 1101, but failed). Henry recognised that many of his subjects including the barons suspected Henry of murdering his elder brother, and saw Robert as the legal heir. Their leader was the Earl of Shrewsbury; Henry seized his lands and banished him. Henry then had to pursue him into Normandy, where the Earl and Robert were raising a force to invade Henry crushed him in battle, and took both him and Robert prisoner, keeping them in captivity for twenty-eight years; the rest of their lives.

Henry had a long argument with the church. Instead of receiving their appointments from the ruling monarch, the bishops and abbots in England wished to receive them from the Archbishop of Canterbury instead. Only when the Archbishop left England in disgust and the Pope threatened to excommunicate the King did Henry agree to their request.

It was seen by the church as an acknowledgement that kings were not necessarily holy or divine.

The border wars with France were a constant source of expense for Henry, who had to raise taxes in England to keep the peace through a large army. He married his son to a neighbouring princess in order to form an alliance; unfortunately his son was drowned a year later when his ship sank in the Channel. Henry then arranged to marry his daughter Maud to someone in the same alliance. All the barons then complained as they saw the kingdom passing to one of England's former enemies upon Henry's death, and went into revolt. Before Henry could do anything about it, he died of a surfeit of lampreys - eating too many eels.

After the death in 1135 of Henry I, his nephew Stephen came to the throne as the barons did not wish to be ruled by a woman, Henry's daughter, Maud. She and her husband Geoffrey of Anjou invaded England from France in 1139, seeking to regain her rightful heritage. Whilst some of the barons eager for personal advancement sided with her against Stephen found now to be a rather weak king others stuck with the throne and a civil war broke out (a popular era these days by the setting of the *Brother Cadfael* stories by Ellis Peters in it). Wide areas of England were devastated; churches were burned for example, St Peter's in Nottingham - or used as strongpoints, personal vendettas proliferated and brother was in some cases set against brother. The Scots and Welsh chose this moment of uncertainty to attack all along their borders, looting and burning the English villages and towns. Many Crown officials and clergy also took this opportunity to feather their own nests as taxes were still collected but never passed on.

King Stephen showed personal bravery in a fight he captured Maud but let her go. She did not return to France but set herself up in Wiltshire and began to rule in her own right, with Stephen ruling from London. The boot went onto the other foot in 1141 as this time Maud took Stephen prisoner she went to London for her coronation but succeeded in only offending the Londoners through being very aloof and extremely high-handed, and who as a result unceremoniously drove her out of the capital. Stephen's wife led his armies in another campaign, which freed him to go after Maud again. She was bottled up in Oxford and only escaped by being lowered from the castle by a rope wearing a white cloak to blend in with the heavy snowfalls. By 1148, Maud had given up any further attempts to gain the throne and left for Normandy, where her husband had succeeded in taking most of Stephen's castles and lands there. In 1153, Stephen acknowledged Maud's son Henry as his heir (who had already made two unsuccessful invasion attempts). For six years in this civil war England had been ravaged by the contending forces, and lawlessness was everywhere.

Henry II was a well-educated man. He inherited a vast kingdom, stretching from the south of France to Hadrian's Wall, which had to be put in order after his fathers loss of grip during the civil wars. He travelled extensively; destroying the castles of any rebel barons, and attacking the Scots pushing them back over the border. He re-established the tax system, sacking anyone who had been lax and introduced trial by jury instead of by combat or ordeal. Once England was put in order, he left with his army for France to do the same there. Only thirteen years of his thirty-five year reign were spent in England.

Henry II is best remembered for a single act the murder of Thomas a Becket. They were close friends, but when Henry appointed Thomas to the post of Archbishop of Canterbury he was astonished that Thomas opposed all his views, being extremely obstinate. They quarrelled; Henry seized Thomas's lands and he had to flee to France. Thomas returned at the order of the Pope in 1170 to excommunicate the priests that had fulfiled the vacant post of Archbishop of Canterbury by crowning Henrys eldest son heir to the throne (by Henrys order). Henry was furious he let slip his infamous mutter, Will no-one rid me of this turbulent priest ?, was overheard by four of his knights who then went straight to Canterbury and killed Thomas in the cathedral. Henry had to do a severe penance; he was whipped by the monks whilst on his knees, and pay for the building of many churches all over England.

It was Henry II that granted Nottingham's Charter in 1155, giving them the rights to hold a twice-weekly market in the square, and he also gave money for the building of a powerful new castle to replace the old wood and earth one, left from the Conquest.

Two of his four sons died including the heir to the throne - leaving Richard and John to feud over the splitting up of Henrys kingdom. Before Henry's death, Richard had allied with the King of France to invade Anjou, Henry's French lands. John joined them when he saw they would succeed. Henry died of a broken-heart at his sons betrayal of him.

During the Third Crusade, Richard I The Lionheart was rarely in England - from a ten-year reign he was in England for only one of them. He was however a popular king, having the then admired qualities of being a born soldier, a powerful warrior, and a charismatic leader of men (although he seemed to use the same technique in his diplomatic relations as with a heavy five-pound axe on the battlefield).

Richard I used the country mainly as a source of funds through the extortionate taxation rates that his brother John is traditionally blamed for - his throne was protected by his Regent and chancellor, William Longechamps. His jealous brother Prince John raised a small force headed by some loyal barons, captured a few castles most notably, Nottingham - marched on London and eventually pushed Longechamps out, electing himself Regent in his brother's absence. Richard after achieving one victory and instigating several massacres of innocent people in the Holy Land - was shipwrecked whilst returning to England, and imprisoned for ransom in a castle near Vienna in Austria by King Leopold. Legend has it that it was Richard's favourite minstrel Blondel who located him, by visiting all the German castles singing Richard's favourite songs, until he heard one day a familiar voice singing in harmony with one.

Whilst the ransom was being collected - in total one whole quarter of the total wealth in England at the time - John approached Philip, the French King, and the castles belonging to Richard in Normandy were seized by the pair of them and shared out equally (it was in trying to recapture these in 1199 that Richard stopped a crossbow bolt and eventually died of blood poisoning). Richard was eventually ransomed, and returned to his kingdom to find it financially poor and also ravaged by famine and starvation. He left again shortly afterwards.

John succeeded to the throne and became king in 1199, becoming one of England's most unpopular monarchs. The French King already had John's measure; he nicknamed him Soft-sword and in 1202 seized the rest of the English possessions in France for himself. He cleverly gave the Normandy estates to Prince Arthur, Richard I's son, the heir to the English throne and having many followers by the fictitious power of his name alone. John had no choice but to fight Arthur for the lands; in a fierce battle, John defeated the French and captured Arthur. Arthur was imprisoned in one of the forts on the Normandy coast, where he eventually disappeared. A rumour circulated that John had him murdered many believed it as Arthur was never seen again, and earned John the additional nickname of *Usurper*.

King John also fell out with the Pope; in naming one of his favourites for the post of Archbishop of Canterbury in 1205 instead of the papal choice for the post, he was excommunicated for nine years in which the Pope forbad the clergy in England to conduct church services or bury the dead in holy ground this resulted in many considering they had relatives consigned to Eternal Perdition due to John's intransigence, and they hated him for it.

John's final mistake and the one he is best remembered for is his heavy taxation of the people. He did introduce charters to major towns and cities, making them independent of feudal barons, allowing them to elect their own officials to run their markets and courts. All this was done for only one reason to create an army of officialdom in which tax collection and the application of his laws could be carried out quickly and efficiently. Coupled with the rather dubious aspects of law at the time, and John's interference in Church affairs, the barons and the Church banded together and drew up a parchment guaranteeing their basic civil rights then and for the future which they expected John to agree to and sign; when he didn't they ran him to earth and the charter was signed at Runnymede on the Thames near Windsor in 1215, becoming known as Magna Carta. A year later, John repudiated the charter and broke all of the promises he'd made by signing it. The barons rose in revolt and England was plunged into civil war again, with the added threat of French invasion. John lost all his wealth trying to cross the Wash at low tide in a manoeuvre to reach London, captured by the French, the tide came in, drowned the horses and submerged the wagons carrying his loot; the casket containing his crown floated out to sea. John was heart-broken; he became ill and died seven days later, in nearby Newark castle.

John was succeeded on the throne by his son, becoming Henry III in 1216. He was crowned in Gloucester, as London was held by the French. There was no crown either - it was never recovered from the sea, no money for the celebrations, and only a few of his supporters turned up for the ceremony. However, enough strong barons did rule well enough on his behalf the French were eventually pushed out of England, and a proper coronation took place in Westminster Abbey. Henry III, along with his father, were not popular kings. Henry III proved to be a bad-tempered spendthrift who drank too much. He carried on attempting his fathers heavy rates of taxation, sent out costly military expeditions to Europe (which all failed), entertained his French wife's greedy relatives and hangers-on lavishly at court, built some expensive palaces and also replaced the royal wardrobe with fine clothes and jewellery. Rebellion was simmering once again.

In 1238, one of the hangers-on, a court favourite of French descent named Simon de Montfort, Earl of Leicester had married Henry's sister but Henry and Simon had argued bitterly ever since about how to govern the country. The disaffected and embittered barons finally asked Simon and his son in 1258 to lead them in revolt; Simon realised that if victorious he would have a chance to rule England in Henry's stead.

After five years of manoeuvring in 1264, the rival forces came together at a battle at Lewes and gave Simon his chance; he captured Henry III and made him swear an oath creating a basic parliament made up of representatives from each county and town in England. The agreement was written out in English (for the first time legal documents up to that time since the Norman Conquest were written in French) and established what would become the House of Commons. The agreement also requested Henry to be more moderate in his expenditure, live within his means and not oppress the merchants and the Poor nor plunder and rob them for the means to furnish supplies for the chieftains castles as had been practiced over the past few years by king, baron, knight and clergy alike!

In 1265, Prince Edward came to his father's rescue and crushed the Simon de Montfort rebels at a battle near Evesham in Worcestershire (only 80 miles from Nottingham, and in one tale Robin Hood and Little John were both there on the side of the rebels). Under summer stormclouds, Prince Edward used a *ruse de guerre* to lure the rebel leaders within range then hacked down the de Montforts, cutting off Simon's head. Many of the defeated rebels took to their heels, fearing a terrible retribution, hiding out in local forests and woods; subsequently outlawed. Under the treaty drawn up by Henry III *The Dictum of Kenilworth* many were outlawed as they didn't or couldn't accept the terms under which they were expected to redeem their confiscated lands. Without funds and living rough, many tried to raise the required cash to buy back their own property by banding together and employing a new stratagem - highway robbery!

Henry III was generous in his later years; whilst Prince Edward ruled, Henry gave gifts such as clothes and shoes, money, wine and Christmas feasts to the Poor. He also gave many gifts of money to abbeys and priories, and founded a hospital in London for women to give birth. His wife, Eleanor of Aquitaine, was generally hated; too many remembered her greedy ways and those of her relatives when she arrived from France in 1235 to marry a husband-king she had never even met. She once threw the Lord Mayor of London into jail until he paid a new tax she introduced in Henry's absence in France; and when sailing in her barge up the Thames she was royally pelted with filth and dirt from the citizens of London standing above her on one of the bridges.

Edward I was another of England's greatest kings. He brought together the lords and the commons for the first time in a parliament and was an excellent soldier. He was a good-looking man, tall and fit, strong and skillful those who knew him well said he was also a bully and unreliable. He had meted out savage retribution for the rebels who had fought against his father with Simon de Montfort, who he had personally slain. It was after this he departed for a grand tour of Europe, returning with his reputation as a great lance in tournaments. It was while he was returning the news arrived of his father's death.

After the coronation, he built a splendid tomb for his father. He then despatched inspectors all over England who were to report back on the state of the nation, when they did return, the news was not good. Edward removed the corrupt officials who had crept back in during his father's reign, and brought in new laws to maintain law and order in an unruly kingdom. Before Edward could apply these, the Welsh and Scots attacked his borders again. The local barons were more interested in acquiring personal gain and feuding with each other than protecting the common folk Edward had to go himself. In 1277 he crushed the self-styled Prince of Wales Llewellyn ap Gruffydd; Edward allowed him to go on calling himself Prince of Wales as long as he agreed to enforce the King's will in what was left the lands he formerly owned that Edward didn't confiscate. Five years later, Llewellyn rebelled again and this time Edward made no mistake - he sent Llewellyn's head back to London for display at the Tower. It was in these Welsh wars that the longbow was first decisively used as a weapon of war.

Edward also threw out the Jews from England, first confiscating their money and property; he built the Welsh castles with it.

In 1296, the Scots rebelled after a heavy tax demand by Edward; who, partly expecting it, despatched his army to Berwick-on-Tweed, sacked it, went onto Dunbar and crushed the Scots army there (using for the first time in warfare a properly constituted body of longbowmen after seeing how decisive they could be from his Welsh campaigns). To show his power over the Scots, he removed their sacred coronation stone from the abbey of Scone and sent it to London. It was not a good move; for years afterwards the army had to be retained in Scotland as small-scale attacks and raids were continuously used against the invaders by the Scots. William Braveheart Wallace (one Scots chronicler naming Wallace the Scottish Robin Hood) fought a long and hard campaign against Edward's forces until being captured; hung, drawn and quartered at Tyburn as a rebel. Edward's troubles weren't over Robert the Bruce now championed the Scots cause, although formerly on the English side; Edward died an old man in 1307 as he was on his way to fight the Scots rebels once again.

Edward was loved by his soldiers, as he dressed in one of their simple uniforms and shared many of their hardships, looking after them as best he could. His last words to them were that his bones be carried into battle until the last Scot had surrendered. They gave him the nickname Hammer of the Scots, and it was carved on his tomb. The border war dragged on for many years to come.

Edward was a bit of a tyrant, during his daughter's wedding he lost his temper and threw her coronet into a fire! He had the first large-scale map of England drawn, and sent explorers to Europe and Asia Minor to gain more knowledge of the outside world. He loved listening to music and stories, and when the fabled King Arthur's grave was discovered at Glastonbury in 1283, served as one of the pall-bearers who carried the body to its new tomb. When Edward's wife died in Nottingham after a forty-year marriage, he was completely distraught; wherever her coffin rested on its way back to London, he built one of the famous Eleanor crosses.

Edward II in 1307 was tall and handsome like his father, but cared nothing for kingship. He liked to enjoy himself in his own pleasures. He gave up the struggle in Scotland, and left the Scots to their own under their newly-crowned king

(Robert the Bruce, in 1306) in order to plan a fresh campaign. He unfortunately managed to upset some of the barons early on, by favouring a French knight named Piers Gaveston, who he married to his niece and made an Earl. He then took the crown jewels from his own wife and gave them to his niece! The English nobles were insulted by the foreigner Gaveston's sneering ways and astonished at him dressing in the royal purple at court; they insisted Edward remove him. He did so, but a few months later, Gaveston was back at court and behaving worse than ever, the barons secretly kidnapped him one night and had him beheaded.

One of the discontented lords was the Earl of Lancaster (Edward's nephew). He refused to help Edward raise an army in 1314 to attack the Scots, with the result that Robert the Bruce and his Scots army - although outnumbered - completely defeated the English at Bannockburn. This brought the Earl of Lancaster to power; whilst Edward languished at court, it was he that ruled England. Personal feuds broke out once more as barons and nobles jostled for places and land, local skirmishes burned village and hamlet, bands of heavily-armed brigands roamed the open country, and a succession of bad harvests due to heavy rain burst rivers and sent hundreds of peasants onto the swampy roads and into the forests searching for food (as one contemporary archivist wrote "the Poor eating dogs, the dung of doves; even their own children".).

Edward within a few years found a new favourite, Hugh Despenser, and once more he began giving land and money to him. Again, the jealous English nobles demanded he be removed, this time Edward was ready for them. He refused the rebels and Lancaster's army was beaten at Borobridge in 1322, Lancaster himself executed. Edward and Despenser were left in a dominant position; until both betrayed by a woman. Isabella, Edward's wife (she earlier lost her jewels) had a secret lover Mortimer, one of the rebel barons. He allied with Isabella's fourteen year-old son, raised an army, and struck. They seized and hanged Despenser and his father, and captured Edward, imprisoning him. In 1327 he was horribly executed by a red-hot poker being thrust up into his body via his anus, so his body could be displayed showing no wounds or facial discolouration from a poison and be seen to have died of 'natural causes'.

Edward III consequently came to the throne very young and very unprepared, in a country ruled in reality by Mortimer and his cronies, the enemies of his father, who they had so cruelly murdered. Edward bided his time; using a secret passage leading into Nottingham Castle (Mortimer's Hole, part of which is still there today) he sent a party of loyal men to surprise Mortimer whilst asleep in bed and carry him off. Edward then hanged him; Queen Isabella was banished to Castle Rising, in Norfolk. Edward then ruled for fifty years; he enjoyed military success (crushing the Scots army in 1333 at Halidon Hill), enhanced the system of pageantry and established an order of chivalry, through a select band of twenty-six of his knights. When Princess Joan's garter dropped off at a ball in Calais, Edward picked it up and handed it back to her, sternly saying to the sniggering onlookers *"Evil be to he, who evil thinks!"* which was then adopted as their motto, and they became The Knights of the Garter; Edward even tried to reconstitute the Knights of the Round Table. Tournaments and jousts were re-organised, rules established and all competitions formally administered; single combats took place, replacing the dangerous and general free-for-all of the past.

The Scots had asked the French for aid against Edward; the French King (although Edward's uncle) was delighted at the opportunity to fuel a fresh rebellion and hopefully in the confusion get what was left of the English possessions in France (with perhaps a bit of England thrown in). Unfortunately, before his plans could be carried out, he died in 1328 without leaving an heir. Edward decided to strike first and attack; he made an immediate claim to the French throne; Philippe VI who had succeeded to it refused to acknowledge Edward's claim. Within ten years Edward had created a vast army and landed in Flanders in 1338; the beginning of The Hundred Years War between England and France.

Edward returned to England in 1340 after a brief campaign and victory; he landed in France again in 1346. The French were better prepared on this occasion and sent a huge army to meet him. At Crecy on the day of the battle, the English longbowmen stepped forth one pace and let fly and by the end of that day thousands of French soldiers were dead, pierced with arrows and lying in heaps. Edward besieged Calais for a whole year, until the town surrendered, the people literally starving to death.

The Scots tried to aid the French by invading in Edward's absence, but the attempt failed; their new king was taken prisoner and sent to Nottingham Castle dungeon, then on to the Tower of London. There followed another campaign in 1356 with Edward's son, The Black Prince, in command. At Poitiers, the then King of France Jean le Bon was captured, and joined the Scots King in the Tower until an enormous ransom was paid. The war dragged on; after a few more years, the French gave into Edward's demands and he received nearly a quarter of France as a result, in return for giving up his claims to the French throne.

A new and less identifiable enemy was now threatening not just England, but the whole of Europe. In the wake of war, came the Black Death. Carried by the brown rat from China, it killed not just Edward III's wife but almost 40% of the population of Europe. It left animals untended, rotting crops not harvested, taxes unpaid and dead bodies lying in the streets of towns as there were no men left alive to drag them to the plague pits; whole villages were decimated, and left abandoned. Edward's soldiers fell in droves, by 1374 they held only Calais on the mainland of France.

It is with this terrible shadow which dominated Europe for over thirty years that we leave the medieval period where the Four Horsemen of the Apocalypse were rarely off-duty and in which Robin Hood was first born. It was just a few short years before the next major conflict struck England the Wars of the Roses, in which the old circle of regicide and terror continued, the curtain coming down at East Stoke near Nottingham in 1487 in the second-bloodiest battle ever fought on English soil (*1).

In well-documented parts of England such as Shropshire, Staffordshire, Yorkshire, Derbyshire and of course Nottingham such as Warsop, Sherwood and Barnsdale, large areas were occupied by brigands and thieves. General discontent still simmered in many places until 1381, coming to a head in the great Peasants Revolt. There was at that time a name prevalent in England - Robin Hood - born sometime during the uncertain, turbulent and rebellious years (many minor local campaigns and three major civil wars) from 1190 until 1272.

In the ballads Robin Hood is in Sherwood Forest when a 'comely King Edward' makes his progress to Nottingham and pardons the outlaws, taking some of them into his service. Edward I; and his son Edward II came to Nottingham in the year 1322 to enquire into raids and robberies within the royal forests and deer parks. Was he the comely Edward of the ballad? One Scots historian writing a history in 1341 placed Robin Hood in it around the year 1266; so maybe not ? More than one historian has Robin and Little John fighting at the battle of Evesham with Simon de Montfort against a cruel king for their rights. Another has proved him to have been in the ranks of Lancaster's army at Borobridge in 1322. Most

Death depicted as an Archer in a medieval woodcut; the yew tree that the bow is made from in celtic mythology represents death and rebirth; and the last month of winter in the old Celtic calendar. Ogham script druidic writing resembles the fletchings on an arrow shaft.

have him trying to secure the ransom for King Richard from the clutches of Prince John, whose supporters are plotting to seize the throne from the rightful King.

Somewhere in a 150 to 200 year period Robin Hood emerged, at first a small spark in a cottage fireside, but fanned into a widespread blaze by hope and belief, finally becoming a fierce beacon for others lost in confusion and dismay to follow - ending as a glowing leading light in the halls of kings.

One of these Robin-Hoods might have been one Roger Godberd. He was born in Leicestershire, and in 1264 at the time of the Simon de Montfort Rebellion was a member of the garrison of Nottingham Castle, and apparently joined the rebels. During the ensuing Baron's War of 1264-5, he had used the opportunity of civil strife to raid nearby Garendon Abbey with a small force and forced the abbot to surrender deeds to land they'd leased from him and bonds for loans of money which he had borrowed, which he presumably destroyed and never repaid. Flushed with this success - he got away with the abbey raid - he went into open rebellion against King Henry in 1267. The following raids became so prolific that for a time Nottingham itself was threatened and the townsfolk forced to cut down forest timber and build palisades and other defences against these predators. The King himself wrote ordering the Sheriff to take firm action against these outlaws, but not naming Godberd himself specifically. Two armed expeditions mounted against them ended in disaster, men and horses being killed.

Five years later, in 1272 - during which time presumably he had still been active in his criminal activities as royal records show a growing count of murders, robberies and raids - Roger Godberd was caught. Reginald de Grey (of Codnor, Notts) had accepted a purse of 100 marks from a pool of money raised in Nottinghamshire, Derbyshire and Leicestershire to catch him. Both Reginald and Roger were members of the Nottingham

Castle garrison of 1264, so Reginald had a distinct advantage that he knew Roger by sight, not just by reputation. He chased him all over Nottinghamshire and Derbyshire into Herefordshire, where he finally laid hands on him. Roger was astonished at this treatment; he pleaded that he thought the King had pardoned him for all that had occurred, as having been necessary in time of war. Roger Godberd was sent to Newgate Prison in London for trial, and was never seen or heard of again. One can speculate what happened to him; but his punishment or death is not documented. Did he get away with that too ?

Another was a Robert Hood, fugitive, a rather ambiguous person listed in the County Rolls of Yorkshire in the year 1230. What fits with Roger Godberd's tale is that we have a Robin Hood, a Sheriff and also a Guy of Gisborne too. Roger Godberd is also said to have been sheltered by several commoners and nobles in Sherwood Forest. In 1322, at the time of the defeat of Lancaster's army, Barnsdale Bar in east Yorkshire was a nest of outlaws, one of whom was a Robert Hood and his wife, Matilda.

The continuing enforcement by the royal foresters of the laws of William I concerning outlaws, poaching and trespass caused many small scuffles. In 1277, two men (both named Robert, of which Robin was then a common nickname, from the Norman French) were arrested in Sherwood by foresters, and locked up in Blidworth village to await trial. That night, over twenty armed men with bows and swords broke into the lock-up, released the two men, beat up the officials, and then left. The case came before the Justices ten years later in 1287, by which time the event had almost been forgotten and most of the culprits, although identified, had disappeared. The three that were arrested in 1287 were soon after released.

Many other such cases exist, not many of the culprits were ever caught and punished. Between the years 1150 and 1400

England was a land of turmoil; rebellion, oppression, lawlessness, pestilence, injustice, brigandry and starvation in which the Law floundered in a sea of uncertainty.

Strangely, an old name for a robber in those days was a *hobbes-hod*.

Footnote
1. There is an excellent publication (1987) available by order through Nottingham Library as a guide outlining the history, location and events of this battle.

Part Nine

Locations in the Legend

Sites in and around Nottingham

"Cupid! Draw back thy bow; and let your arrow Go-oh ."
Sixties popular song

If you study any Ordnance Survey map of England, Scotland or Wales, it is hard not to find at least one reference to Robin Hood. Nowhere is he more noted than in Nottinghamshire, and in particular Sherwood Forest around Edwinstowe. A local road sign near my present home declares 'Nottinghamshire; Robin Hood Country' to passing motorists entering the county.

I counted in passing when I first came to live here over a hundred sites or landmarks associated with Robin Hood, then gave up and concentrated only on the thirty or so firmly connected with the established legend. Once collected and mapped, I used my bicycle to visit them on day-tours and fit each of them into the stories.

Some undoubtably are flagrant additions to the stories for financial gain, others are traceable to the May Games and Morris Dance, others have a connection tenuous at best. But the best of them, visited in company with a guide who knows the legends, is an enjoyable day out indeed in a wonderful county of great natural beauty.

Well, let's begin at Nottingham Castle.

Nottingham Castle

Richard III raised his Standard here at the end of the Wars of the Roses, before going off across the old Trent Bridge to Bosworth Field to lose both his crown and his life. Charles I raised his flag here too, at the beginning of the English Civil Wars; the same high winds that made life in the castle miserable blew it down three times, and it was taken as a fearful omen. King John spent a lot of time here in the absence on Crusade of his brother Richard, and at the Hunting Palace near Clipstone.

The original castle was a mound atop the high crag with a palisade of wooden stakes around it, defended from the south by the River Leen curling around its base. This was replaced by stone walls in 1170, built by Henry I; Henry II began the first stone castle here, and by the late 13th Century it appeared a powerful stronghold but had an inherent fault the local stone used to build it. Richard I on his return from the Crusades appeared unannounced here one day demanding admittance - the garrison in disbelief told him what he could do with himself; after a short siege he gained entry and hanged most of them in a fit of pique.

A local folk-tale tells of an existing curse upon the castle due to the hanging of some young Welsh boys held as hostages there from the battlements by his brother, Prince John. Edward I built most of the existing great round watchtowers and castle remains, but if you stand in the moat or on the Castle Green you can get an impression (depending on your

Nottingham Castle, a superb model of the old castle at the height of its power in AD1500; on display at the castle

imagination) of the sort of strongpoint any Robin Hood might have seen; a model of the castle in the museum circa AD1500 will serve those without this facility. The numbers of soldiers in the garrison averaged about one hundred, made up of foot and archers; around fifty household servants and workers would also have been housed here.

The solid rock the castle stands on is honey-combed with tunnels and caves for storage; more are found at regular intervals, and some of them date back to prehistoric times. Little remains of the castle and the great open baileys any Robin Hood might have seen. The old castle was used as a stronghold again, but destroyed with gunpowder and pick by the garrison after the end of the English Civil Wars. It was already a ruin before that conflict as the unsuitable sandstone used to create it was by then in a very sorry state of repair, being held by the garrison as best they could, as a strongpoint denying any use of the town and guarding the passage of the mighty River Trent by Royalist forces. Two heavy cannon were emplaced to fire at the bridgehead south of the castle.

The building before you today here is the late 17th Century palladian-style mansion built for the Duke of Newcastle, burned in its dereliction in the 1830s by Chartist rioters and is now Nottingham Museum and Art Gallery. The top of the original castle rock would have been where the roof of the present building is today, and was lowered to allow a more extensive groundplan for the building than would have then permitted. High winds and gales always made life up here a cold and draughty affair, as the odd window being sucked out still proves today !

An important building near here is the Tryppe To Jerusalem Inn (1189AD) at the base of the castle rock. It is said to be the oldest inn in England (*Tryppe* is old English for 'halt'; crusaders on their way to the Holy Land stopped here for refreshment). Robin Hood may well have occasionally indulged here too! Local folk tales have it that the dusty old ship - now in a glass case still complete with dust - hanging in the upstairs bar was possessed by a nasty evil spirit who ensured a sticky end for the last two people who touched it. During the inn's renovations in late 1997, a local spiritualist was called in to move the ship and cast a spell protecting the inn and its occupants. It seemed to have worked until Boxing Day when the south facing castle wall fell off into Canal Street. The spirit would not be denied its vengeance !

The 14th century gatehouse of the castle was in recent times extensively rebuilt, based on the original lines and using some of the existing foundations; a great stone arch and pavement however replaced the drawbridge. Instead of Guardrooms, one side of the Gatehouse is used for the castle souvenir shop, and the other for the modern Sheriff of Nottingham when entertaining his Public. Below it the court - where Will Scarlett was once due to be hanged by the Sheriff but was rescued by Robin and the lads is where the statue of Robin Hood now stands, with bronze plaques around it on the castle walls depicting events in the legend.

The dark confines of Sherwood Forest would have been visible easily from the high keep of the castle, stretching away northwards in a rolling green tide over hill and down dale as far as the naked eye could see. A private hunting area lay just to the west of the castle, the origins of the exclusive modern Park district of Nottingham, where even today the gates across the roads allowing access are traditionally and ceremonially shut on occasion to keep the rabble out and maintain the present residents status.

Nottingham Town

Henry II granted the towns charter in 1155, establishing two weekday markets in the square. Originally a wall ran across the square separating the Norman castle hill from the Saxon hill to the east. The markets were held here; Robin Hood once sold his wares here to the Sheriff's wife masquerading as a potter (or meat disguised as a butcher) in a rather deep and risky plan to trick the Sheriff into the forest where he could be detained and entertained all at his own expense, of course!

The Sheriff of the town would have lived in The Red Lodge formerly at the end of Angel Row, at one end of Market Square not in the castle, as that was the sole domain of the Constable of Nottingham Castle. As you pass out of the town going north, you are in old Sherwood Forest as soon as you cross Upper Parliament Street, along which the town walls once ran.

To the east of the square in the historic Lace-Market area is St Mary's Church, where Robin once desperately went to mass after a two-week lay off, was recognised by a priest who reported him to the Sheriff, leading to his capture. The body of the man (or men) in one story Robin slew and first became an outlaw may be here too, as recent excavations showed. St Mary's was a religious site well before the coming of the Normans; the old Saxon church was incorporated into the Norman one, and in 1474 that too was built over and demolished, leaving the church you see today. See if you can spot The Green Man !

St Peter's Church further into town was taken over by William Peveril (see later), who gave it to the monks at Lenton priory. St Peter's Church was the scene of an unfortunate massacre in 1140 when the castle was attacked by the Earl of Gloucester. The citizens sheltering here were all slaughtered; a fire was then started which burned down St Peter's and then Bridlesmith Gate too. The church was later rebuilt.

Out to the north-east is the old St Ann's Well, where visitors in the 17th and 18th centuries were invited to sit in Robins chair whilst wearing his cap and holding his bow, and drink the waters - this initiation ceremony earned you the right to be a full member of the Brotherhood of Robin Hood. The name Robin Hoods Well is recorded in the year 1500, and is also supposed to have healing qualities. The well - first noted in 1287, and known as Owswell, near Robin Hood Chase - fell into disuse, was covered over and the location lost. It was rediscovered by accident in 1987 in the back yard of a public house; it was then covered over and waits patiently today for the funding to reopen it. In AD1195, according to an old city document seen by Mr Jim Lees, an affray occurred here, by Robin Hood and his marauders. The case was dismissed, as a local nobleman from Lincolnshire made a plea in mitigation on behalf of the defendants, who were then let off. Unfortunately this singularly important document has recently disappeared.

North along Mansfield Road lies Church Rock cemetery. Three large caves here with graves lying on top of and around them, are also named for Robin Hood.

Sherwood Forest

Sherwood Forest was known as Scyriud in AD958. After the Conquest, William I made it all a royal preserve for hunting. The first mention of Sherwood by name is in 1154, concerning a case of trespass under the Bishop of Durham; managed previously by a chap named William Peveril for the purposes of royal hunting. In 1218, the area of Sherwood Forest was laid down by a survey under Henry III, around 19000 acres in all, covering twenty miles in length and about five miles broad. The northern boundary was the river Meden, the southern the river Leen; it contained three deer parks which were enclosed by a palisade Nottingham, Clipstone and

Bestwood. The forest was mostly oak and birch, elm and yew. In it lay many dales (areas of open ground) and over twenty villages like Sutton, Kirkby, Edwinstowe and Blidworth. For the purposes of hunting, Clipstone Park was served by the royal hunting palace there, and Bestwood Park by a lodge within the park itself.

The forests were maintained and administered by a group of foresters, agisters and verderers who carefully oversaw the provision and allocation of game, firewood, timber and grazing. By the year 1190 due to encroachment by villages and farming these officials really began to tighten up William the Conqueror's forest laws (introduced in 1066) causing a good bit of bad feeling amongst the locals who had come to regard the forests as a right rather than a privilege at that point. It became a serious crime to be caught taking firewood, hunting game with hound or arrow, or removing timber from the forest. The locals took care not to get caught, and the war between poacher and gamekeeper which still goes on today began. Between 1200AD and 1400AD the forest was extremely popular with England's royalty and saw many visits for the purposes of hunting and sport.

The building of ships for the Royal Navy which began in the time of Henry VIII reduced all the old oak forests of England. Many famous old oaks survive, the best known being The Major Oak. The name Major Oak originates from Major Hayman Rook, a noted local historian. The tree was formerly known as the Queen's Oak - for no other reason than it was the biggest lady in the forest; and after that the Cockpen or Cockpit Tree in the 17th and 18th centuries, as a cock-fighting pit was erected under its branches, and the hollow interior as a coop to house the fighting cocks. The tree itself is between 800 and 1500 years old; nobody can agree ! It is famous as being one of the trysting places of Robin Hood, and the site of his main camp. Legend has it that Robin on many occasions hid inside its hollow trunk as the Sheriff's men combed the forest seeking him. The old coach-way for visitors coming to see the tree in the nineteenth century is still visible in parts. During WW2, Sherwood Forest was an enormous ammunition dump, and a railway serving it ran past the Major Oak. In attempting to destroy the site, a Nazi bomber once dropped four bombs all of which failed to explode, falling in the nearby Thoresby Hall Estate.

Another trysting tree used by Robin Hood said to be two thousand years old was felled by the "Sheriff's Men" of West Riding County Council despite a great local protest in the village of Todwick in 1961 to permit the building of an old folks home. The modern tree bearing the plaque is a sapling of the Major Oak, planted in 1974 to replace the original.

At the same time in Sherwood, another great old oak Robin Hood's Larder, was blown down by the great gales of 1960. Stories exist of the Merry Men hanging their game inside it, possibly to smoke it for storage. The original name of the tree was the Butcher's Oak. The Parliament Oak stands near Edwin's Cross on the Mansfield Road, where in 1212 King John summoned a parliament after the revolt in Wales. Another summons went forth in 1290, when Edward I summoned his nobles here, and met at the royal hunting lodge at Clipstone.

The Greendale Oak died in the late 18th Century, after a local landowner cut a passage ten feet high by six feet wide through it to allow a coach and horses to go through. Another great tree now dead - stood where West Gate, Mansfield now stands. A plaque there claims to mark the centre of the Royal Forest. The Pilgrim Oak stands at the entrance to Newstead Abbey on the modern main road. Lord Byron climbed it, and sat under it writing his poetry. It was his reputation in history that prevented this tree being felled in the seventies. Many old stag-headed oaks still stand; you can see them as you make your way through the forest.

Blidworth and Fountain Dale

St Mary's churchyard at Blidworth, contains a stone under some yew trees which was once part of the tower of the old church. It marks where, nearby, Will Scarlett is buried. Will Scarlett in one tale is Robin's nephew, to a sister living in Mansfield. Part of the relics from the old church stand close by. Will's grave was against the wall of the old church. The new church holds the ancient Rocking Ceremony for the child born nearest to Christmas day each year. The child is dressed in old garments and placed in a ceremonial crib inside the church. A nearby bench was placed in the graveyard here by the comrades of a brave soldier of the 3rd Parachute Regiment as a memorial to him.

A cottage once reputedly stood in the village which was where Maid Marian stayed, waiting for Robin Hood to arrive and take her off to Edwinstowe on their wedding day. A cave here was another storage area for the Merry Men, hiding food and treasure from the Sheriff's men. Blidworth is a likely spot for the old ale house where Robin Hood, Little John and others of the band called regularly for a drink of old October and to pick up any information about travellers or news from the landlord.

A great Druid's Stone stands in a nearby field. Local legend has it of one of the places where Druids practiced their religion. It is all that remains of deposits from a mighty stream emanating from a glacier in the last 100,000 years how it escaped being called Robin Hood's Stone or similar I cannot imagine! There is a hole through it which has bred several local tales of hole-y stones. The rock it stands on is the same Bunter Pebble Bed that makes Robin Hoods Hills at Annesley, and Nottingham Castle perches on top of.

The view over towards Blidworth village from Blood and Guts Lane

The Druid Stone near Blidworth

The Little John public house on the lane to Larch Farm stands at the head of a lane locally named Blood and Guts. We will pass along it as it is the lane leading to the stream where Robin Hood and Little John had their legendary meeting, ending with Robin taking an early bath in the stream after a fight with quarterstaffs.

The old Saxon moat near here used to mark where an ancient shrine once stood, manned by hermits, who lived in the nearby sanctuary at the well. Friar Tuck was one of these hermits; Robin and Tuck in a battle of wits first carried each other on their backs across this moat, ending in Robin being baptised by Tuck in the water. The monks of Newstead Abbey are said to have placed a curse on the moat, which was supposed to have removed the water from it. According to local legend, water only appears in it every seven years. The monks (being good Christians) would not of course be using curses this is another reflection on the power of the New Religion being used against the Old Religion, and is still seen today in the revival of Water Well-dressing over in Derbyshire, where the old water spirits were christianised. A sluicegate still stands in the moat; a good view can be had by walking a few yards on where the Robin Hood Way turns off to the left. The hermitage and well are rather dilapidated since an old beech tree fell on them some years ago. No water now flows here but it was rather soggy during one of my visits in 1998. A ghost said to be Sir Walter Scott walks regularly through here and has been seen by occupants of nearby Fountain Dale House, where Sir Walter penned part of Ivanhoe. The house, behind which is an old coach house, is in parts dated to earlier than 1275 and contains a priests hole in an upstairs room. (The house and grounds are private property today, so no trespassing please!)

West of here is Thieves Wood, where Robin Hood and the boys once drove out a nest of particularly pestiferous robbers plaguing the locals. Friar Tuck sent for Robin as the robbers

A rebuilt section of the old ruins in Blidworth cemetery where Will Scarlet is buried

King John's Palace near Clipstone

had kidnapped a young girl and robbed her father the girl was rescued and the fathers purse returned. The robbers no doubt came to a sticky end. Nearby Bishops Wood is said to be named after the Bishop of Hereford of the ballads, stopped here by Robin Hood and his wealth transferred to a more needy population.

Clipstone

Clipstone was the site of a medieval royal hunting lodge. Prince John stayed here a lot, and the site became known as King John's Palace. It was built originally as a church by the King Edwin of Northumbria and later extended by Henry I into the palace that John would have known. Robin Hood and his band are supposed to have entered it and released the prisoners in the dungeons after luring the king and his men away to the caves of Cresswell in a fruitless search for them. It was destroyed by a fire in 1220, but rebuilt by Henry III in 1270. The remains of the lodge are now preserved as a national monument (another hunting palace site lies nearby at Kinghaugh). Close by is another old tree, the Parliament Oak. This is where Edward I summoned an important parliament in 1290; John had done the same in 1212. Richard The Lionheart met William, the Lion King of Scotland here in 1194, when they no doubt had a good growl at each other due to stretched diplomatic relations. Nearby stood the (now demolished) cottage claimed to be the home of Little John; as one John Naylor, a nailmaker.

On the road to Edwinstowe, you pass The Archway House, a picturesque folly built in 1842. It is decorated with statues of Robin Hood, Little John and Maid Marian, King Richard I and Alan-a-Dale. Nearby Thoresby Hall also has fine wooden carved statues of Robin Hood and Little John next to a large fireplace.

Annesley

Annesley Hall is best recently known for the crashed UFO of the 1980s but before that for its connection with Lord Byron, who stayed here and used an old garden door as a target for his soldierly pistol practice! The nearby outcrops of stone on Robin Hoods Hills here is named Robin Hoods Seat, from the outlaws habit of sitting here watching for likely targets also - in the form of rich travellers - riding the main highroad. Robin Hoods Cave disappeared in the mid-19th century, after being used to store dynamite by workmen working on the nearby railway cutting. All that remains is a slight hollow - or should I say crater ? - on the hillside.

There are the remains of a Norman motte and bailey castle near here, perhaps the ancestral home of the knight Sir Richard of the Lea in the ballads; at Annes-Lea ?

Papplewick Village

St James Church here contains many graves of past foresters, showing their bows, arrows and hunting horns on the tombslabs of the aisle. In the ballads, Robin Hood saved a young girl named Ellen from an arranged marriage to an aged nobleman here, and so earned him the undying loyalty of her true love, Alan-a-Dale - and the enmity of her father !

Papplewick was the headquarters in this period for the Kings Foresters; the churchyard has some ancient yews perhaps encouraged and nurtured to supply future bowstaves ? A local tale has bowyers cutting staves from them for this purpose.

In the churchyard lies the grave of one of Lord Byron's faithful retainers, who died in 1822. A medieval main road, the Kings Great Way, passed here (a portion still remains going off towards Newstead Abbey) and gave rise to many

Robin Hoods Stables near Papplewick

local stories of Robin Hood. A nearby cave, Robin Hoods Stables, is said to be where Robin kept two fast horses for his or others use requiring speed up or down the highway. It could in fact have been a medieval hermitage as the modern name implies it is a spacious, dry dwelling, and three cut-outs inside could serve as mangers for feed (the owners of the property in the 1970s kept two horses here). It stands only 150 yards from the old medieval highway (on private property).

Edwinstowe

This village is the spiritual home of Robin Hood. Each year it is crowded with visitors as for three days during the school holidays the Robin Hood Festival is staged here, centred around the Major Oak and the Sherwood Forest Visitor Centre. Merry Men and outlaws - when not cheering on the mounted jousters, giving period archery displays or telling tales of Robin Hood - walk the streets of Edwinstowe once more; lurking on street corners, eyeing the local girls, eating fish and chips out of newspaper, and of course quaffing the local brew sitting by the fountain outside their favourite inn opposite the St Mary's church, the Maid Marian!

The village received its name as the burial place of Edwin, the first Christian king of Northumbria (converted by his wife, Ethelburga). He died in battle in 633AD a few miles away at Hatfield. His headless body was brought by his faithful attendants and buried in a clearing in the forest, now under St Mary's Church. A memorial cross and plaque lies further up the road toward Mansfield, down a track off to the right; a nearby hermitage was occupied from ancient times by a succession of priests, whose task it was to pray for the existing monarch. St Mary's Church itself is part of the penance laid on Henry II for unfortunately instigating the murder of Thomas a Becket, as are many others all over the

Edwinstowe Church

St Mary's Church, Edwinstowe; a view of the church today
which was built on top of the site of Edwin's grave (AD 633)
and the later Saxon church

147

country. Inside, along the aisle there are carved heads, two of which in local folklore are suppose to be Henry and Thomas glaring across at each other for eternity ! Two other carved heads are of interest; a strange bearded man, and a strange symbolic effigy that harks back to pagan times.

St Mary's church in Edwinstowe is where Robin Hood and Maid Marian had their marriage under the greenwood tree (only a short walk away) sanctified and blessed. A new statue of Robin and Marian was unveiled in July 1998 outside the library on the High Street. The village existed in 1066 as part of the Royal Saxon manor of Maunsfield. In 1334 the Vicar of St Mary's was convicted of forest trespass, and of killing the Kings deer !

There are many splendidly evocative forest walks around Edwinstowe. One of them passes The King's Stand, an medieval earthwork where the King and his invited guests would wait bow and arrow in hand, while the foresters drove deer towards them to shoot at. You can drop off the car in any of the carparks around here and walk for miles through what remains of one of England's most ancient woodlands. The Forest Rangers stage many interesting events throughout the year, all published in a small booklet; from exploring the flora and fauna, to staging medieval murder mysteries and a torchlit spooky Halloween search for lost ghosts !

Nearby Wellow has a unique village green, complete with a tall maypole. An old ruined castle of the 12th century lies within a half-mile; a defensive ditch of some magnitude surrounded the entire medieval village. St Swithin's Church here is well worth a visit, as some of the oldest and finest yew trees in England grow here; a local folktale has Robin Hood making a bowstave from one of them. Was fortified Wellow one of Robin Hood's strongholds in case of real emergency ?

Mansfield

A Royal Manor in the medieval period, with a castle of sorts, and another priory. Will Scarlet is reputed to have been born here, as one William Gamwell, to Robin Hood's sister. A plaque in the town states that spot marks the centre of Sherwood Forest.

Barnsdale in Sherwood

Mr Jim Lees, noted Nottingham historian and chronicler of Robin Hood, makes a detailed examination and case for Barnsdale being the haunt of Robin Hood - not being the area to the north of here which carries its name, but in a dale closer to Nottingham and most likely to be the place where Robin Hood lurked in close proximity to Nottingham and enjoyed the provision of game, water and local support whilst standing against the Sheriff. Jim's case certainly makes sense. Despite the feeling you get from the legends that Robin had wings and flew from adventure to adventure with astonishing speed over the counties of Nottingham, Derbyshire and Lincolnshire, a location such as Barnsdale being where Jim places it supported by documents and reasoning is sound. It stands between both main roads of the era, has a good stream running through it, and is just far enough away from Nottingham to be out of reach of the Sheriff, but close enough to be a severe annoyance to him. If you have to retire and disperse if heavily threatened, then there are three good bases within a half days march to regroup, then strike back at the enemy who is now far from home and deep within your forest. Jim puts Barnsdale the old Bryunsdale, Bernesdale, Bruinsdale or Brinnesdal on old maps - at the junction of the Day Brook (the old Depe Brook) and the river Leen, in the modern districts of Basford and Sherwood, just adjacent to the royal deer park of Bestwood where I currently live.

Nearby Bestwood Park still has plenty of old trees. The modern lodge a bar and restaurant is on the site of the older one, and a nearby ancient mounting block for horsemen carries the iron plaques of 1878 commemorating the 1650 survey, a description of how the entire hunting park and lodge were given by Charles II as a gift to his favourite orange-seller, Nell Gywn.

Kirklees Priory

This is the site associated with the death of Robin Hood. Robin Hood has been forgiven by the King, and after serving at his court for a while, decides that life in the greenwood wasn't so bad after all, and returns there. Whilst feeling unwell, the now ageing Robin Hood leaves Sherwood with Little John despite the protestations of his band, and goes off to a priory for medical attention. Despite a timely warning from a strange wise-woman they meet, the two men continue on their way. For some reason revenge, reward or personal feud the prioress is told of or recognises Robin, and in concert with a lover / friend / relative recommends bleeding for Robin by opening a vein in his arm and letting out a small amount of blood (a common treatment for disorders in this period). The accomplice bores a small hole in a pewter vessel to catch the blood, and stands it by the bed on a larger vessel. The smaller vessel never fills up with his blood as it seeps through the hole into the larger one, and Robin loses so much blood he becomes so weak as to prevent recovery or assist "assassination".

When the plot is finally exposed Robin prevents Little John burning the place down and killing both murderers as one is a woman (whose sex he is sworn to respect - although she later , in one story, committed suicide when confronted with her guilt), kills the male accomplice Red Roger / Roger of Doncaster - and then asks Little John to help him shoot a final arrow, the place where it falls in the nearby wood to become his final resting place (about 650 yards away from the place where he reputedly died in Little John's arms).

In another tale, the perpetrators poison Robin Hood, in a lethal dose mixed with a tincture or cordial. The gravesite nearby of Elizabeth de Staynton is locally held to be the woman that betrayed Robin Hood; in this tale the prioress is Robin's aunt or cousin, and her lover a relation of the then diseased bugbears of Robin Hood, the Sheriff of Nottingham or Guy of Gisborne. This tale partly explains why Roger is there out for revenge in a blood-feud. Roger the deceased accomplice only appears in the stories at this point. His inclusion and ill-will toward Robin appears only to provide a necessary revenge focus; Robin or John due to their personal codes can't obviously kill a woman, but somebody has obviously got to be seen to be sliced up and left for the dogs in revenge for Robin's demise !

A large graveslab here bears a epitaph to Robin, but has been the centre of controversy for years as to whether or not it is genuine, or even moved here from another location. It may, of course, have been added later; the possession of saintly relics was a great boon to any religious house. The inclusion in the story of a vessel used to catch Robin's blood may be a link with earlier stories; of the cup that was used at the Last Supper the sacramental Holy Grail.

Robin Hood's longbow today at Renishaw Hall moved from Kirklees Hall in the late 1600s, having been passed down from generation to generation as such. In a tourist booklet of 1700, it resided for a time at Fountains Abbey.

Religious Sites: Rufford Abbey, Lenton Abbey, Welbeck Abbey & Newstead Abbey

Now ruined, nevertheless in Norman times Rufford and Lenton were two extremely important and wealthy religious sites. Lenton Abbey stood near an important road, used by Little John in one of the ballads; but is also ruined, only fragments remaining.

Newstead Abbey was a home for Augustinian monks from the 12th century. Rufford Abbey was Cistercian, dating back to 1147, and not a popular place with the locals, as the monks seemed set on grabbing all the land in sight, supported by the nobles; nowadays a country park, and the home of the Nottinghamshire Tourist Office. Further north, Welbeck Abbey was founded as a monastery in the 12th century. There was also a priory in nearby Worksop, begun in 1145; the new church there is unique in having the only wayside shrine in England, built in 1314. The Kings Great Way the important road north from Nottingham would have seen a lot of traffic carrying finance and statute from these abbeys, through Sherwood Forest; easy pickings for Robin Hood !

Nearby Southwell has a beautiful Minster, also begun in the 12th Century (once again look for the Green Man !). It was at the Saracens Head public house in Southwell that Charles I was taken into captivity by Parliament, prior to his subsequent execution some years later. A guided scenic and informative walk around Southwell is provided by the local history group.

It is impossible to visit all the sites - even in this area - associated with Robin Hood in a week. I often call in on one of them in passing, and record them photographically. In speaking to local folk, you often at the same time pick up a few tips as to legend or fact. There are also sites well worth not seeing, and also require a long-distance trek to reach. Some sites have also disappeared in living memory - I asked on a recent visit about two stones in a field near Whitby marking two arrow shots made by Robin and Little John from the abbey there have now been removed, and the fields in which they once stood are ear-marked for housing development. An aged friend recalls in his youth seeing two stones marking the same feat at the head of Whitby harbour, now also evidently gone. The tale of Robin Hood and his defeat of the Viking Pirates at nearby Ravenscar (the Black Raven was the Viking pirate flag), told to me by an enthusiastic local resident where it actually really happened at Robin Hood's Bay was both entertaining and amusing. It was pouring with rain outside, and the beer was very good !

That story occurs before 1060, before the Norman Conquest; could the comely King Edward of the ballad have been Edward the Confessor ?

A Norman knight in a bad temper; he's not happy when he's hungry ! (Spirit of England)

Summary

"When Adam delved and Eve span
Who then was the Gentleman?"

Part of a sermon preached during the Peasant's Revolt by
John Ball, the mad priest of Kent, on 13th June 1381

The Church these days gives an acknowledgement and
sanction to Robin Hood because of his Christian qualities - an
odd paradox, he never made sainthood but he is considered
the patron saint of Archery; nobody ever sees a traditional
archer anywhere without unconsciously thinking of Robin
Hood! We have seen how real persons can make the transition
from reality to folklore; how easier is it to do the same in
reverse? The Legend of Robin Hood makes a clear statement
in that respect. In Nottingham today, I counted ninety
references in shop signs and such in thirty minutes alluding
to Robin Hood.

Nottingham was jokingly referred to by a leading policeman
as Robin Hood Country when the crime figures were released
in 1996 and Nottingham was seen as the UK crime capital for
thefts of personal property! In only two countries in the world
does a legend of a Robin Hood character not exist (the USA
and Canada - although you can consider Davy Crockett and
Hiawatha one closer parallel exists in native American
folklore). The ancient Greeks had their super-heroes Achilles
and Hercules, and the Swiss of course have William Tell.

A lion-heart suffering a coronary at present-day Nottingham Castle!

They 'named no names' in old England; many assumed a new one, or got given a nickname. For those in such outlaw bands and 'on the run', anonymity was sometimes necessary in case of future capture and torture, involving a friend or a family in the shame of a public execution after trial - executions which were often a public spectacle and very savage. But an 'outlaw' in medieval days was not necessarily a rogue and a thief; in two medieval cases come to light, men became 'outlaws' without even knowing they had, only finding out later. They had an instant right of appeal to the allegations that made them 'outlaws', but it was sometimes lost in the 'fudge'. In law after *Magna Carta*, no longer were men guilty before trial, and 'outlaws' were treated decently when caught until proved guilty at a trial, and not thrown into the nearest dark dungeon to rot *per se* (although well-known rogues and robbers guilty of murders still ran that risk if caught).

'Outlaws' may just be men standing 'falsely accused' without benefit of trial, in debt (a common trait of 'gentlemen' in history) or merely 'absent without leave' from where they should be. Some were simply what society might label today 'drop-outs'. They were often good people, who were sheltered and helped by their friends or by local folk who extended a kind hand to them in their difficulties. It would take an extraordinary man to survive for many years in one area just on what he could steal in large quantities from the locals, who would not give up their belongings for long on an everlasting basis without receiving something in return - this sort of 'survival of the fittest' is always based on a nomadic existence.

Starving to death on a diet of pure protein in the form of animals from the power of your aim is not in the long-term beneficial to health, our daily bread (or a suitable substitute for it) is an essential part of survival; it can't be shot at and got with an arrow and does not grow on trees, but is the result of settled and careful agriculture by someone. Robin Hood existed in *partnership* with the locals. They helped feed and maintain him, and he paid them back in kind by protecting them or dropping off the occasional 'tax rebate'. They also probably fed him *information* - vital in this sort of existence - where you survive by knowing as much about your enemy and the terrain as about yourself. In one ballad, Robin Hood eliminates a band of robbers lurking in a local wood near Sherwood Forest who are preying on the locals. They are Robin's 'locals', and the thieves are quickly sent packing or if they won't go, exterminated. Robin can't afford to lose the help of his 'locals'.

Robin is the archetypal hero; good with children and old folk, dealing with common men and kings, physically strong and a deadly fighter but cunning too, both witty in his dealings and fair in judgement. Like every good man, he has a good woman behind him. He is well respected by his colleagues, and has a circle of firm - and like him, charitable - friends, who offer advice which he considers before making his decision. He sets an example to us all; he fights not for personal gain but for 'fun' and the Right, and he knows he *is* right too; he has great wealth and yet is not a 'material person'. He has a sense of humour, an air of 'innocence', a twinkle in his eye, and a spring in his step. He is extremely charming the accosted wayfarers in the ballads that manage to beat him in a fight, all end up joining his band and giving him their love and respect. His clothes are simple homespun or leather, nothing fancy (except as a disguise). He respects women, has no vices and doesn't drink to excess when in society of which his own particular circle he loves. He is not a lord or an earl, but a simple yeoman living in the woods; one of us, mixing with the highest and lowest alike.

He even makes kings look to their crowns by pointing out their 'duty' to live for the commoners - not vice versa; Henry VIII (a skilled archer himself, and 'fan' of Robin Hood) used him on at least one occasion to justify the Dissolution of the abbeys and monasteries due to their graft). Should one of the

Sheriffs *posses de commitatus* enter the greenwoods, this matter is often resolved not in personal combat man-to-man by the outlaws but with a few well-aimed arrows; but he will fight and can fight - to the death if he has to, and often temporarily loses his temper doing so!

To many, he is the *essence* of the 'Englishman'; the philosophy of Might is Right promoted by a man or men in armour riding rough-shod over the peasants or by Royal Decree never existed in the forests occupied by Robin Hood. Sherwood is just another name for Shangri-la as was Camelot. All three are known as havens or refuges for those seeking sanctuary for whatever reason; if his men don't immediately recognise this new democracy or require guidance in the very brutal age they live in as to how they will conduct themselves as part of his band, he sets them simple rules to follow so they do. The longbow - and particularly its mate, the crossbow - were subjected to later 'controls' as they were seen as the potential weapons of assassins; an arrow from Robin Hood or the Merry Men is seen as a final, swift and accurate form of justice; judge, jury and executioner all rolled into one for someone who always richly deserves it! Even the King himself pardons Robin and his men when they eventually meet; probably as he had no other choice as Robin couldn't be caught by the forces of law and order and by that time is regarded by the commoners as God-sent anyway. If you can't beat them, get them to join you!

Robin Hood offers above all Hope and Freedom *if* you are the right sort of chap with no family, responsibility or obligation; debts or cares - to reach out into the forest and take his hand. But is it just *Faery* all over again? Whatever, this appeal has lasted so far over 800 years.

If Robin Hood had *never* existed, someone would have invented him. He will never fade now as long as there are oaks in Sherwood, bows and arrows, children - and merry men, like me - and a basic human inclination in spirit to be better and bigger than we are. King Arthur himself in English legend stands second to Robin Hood; in a poll conducted some years ago to find out who was the most popular man in history, Robin Hood came second only to Jesus Christ (and with whom Robin is also strongly associated in certain quarters).

We will *never* know who Robin Hood was; the man who began it all, the very first. Preceding men may have founded willingly or unwillingly the basic tales; later men (including the Kymes, Foliots and FitzOoths) may have been included or even supplanted them. Some answers to later legends perhaps lie not with Robin Hood himself, but with someone who did exist, whose activities are officially recorded and documented - his greatest adversary, the Sheriff of Nottingham. The layers added to the basic legend of Robin Hood by succeeding historians and researchers, each seeking to verify - or debunk - those preceding them have almost at times obscured it from view.

The ballads and stories attributed to and of Robin Hood have been changed and adapted so often since their conception can be interpreted now almost anyway anyone likes, as we've already seen, by portraying Robin as a fallen knight of chivalry, a social rebel or a cut-throat brigand. The original form is now probably almost lost; but I personally think we are *closer* to it today than ever before. I met a few debunkers whilst researching this; I found them to be people who fell into one of two categories - a) those so enmeshed in modern materialism that they badly *needed* Robin Hood; or b) definitely 'Sheriff's Men' - and badly needing one of his arrows! They are vastly outnumbered by the growing numbers of 'Robin Hood's' who in the face of the ecological threats to our forests and disappearing greenbelts, have taken up arms in their own little way to hit a lick against 'Norman' industrialists and developers !

The first man - Adam - was said to be made in the likeness of God; Robin Hood has been created *by* us and *for* us in a constantly changing image to suit our needs; hence there is a little bit of everyone inside Robin Hood; and a little bit of Robin Hood inside everyone too.

There is so much to read and find out about Robin Hood, with opinions and views from all angles and depths, and numerous stories by authors interpreting the old tales in their own way to make them 'fit'. I cannot list all the books available - many of which are now extremely hard to find - but they are all excellent reading and the search for them is half the fun !

In the ballad stories, it is 'Church Lees', 'Kirkley' or 'Kirkesley' named as the place where Robin Hood died. Did this become *Kirklees* in later oral telling or in the printing of the ballads? Was it fact Kirkby - near Mansfield, in Sherwood Forest - where Robin Hood really died? Or is it at Annesley, (Annes-lea?) one of the possible sites for the home of Sir Richard of the Lee, the poor knight Robin Hood helped back onto his feet, adopted by one later writer as the father of Maid Marian? A hitherto unknown tale I recently 'unearthed' has the remains of Robin Hood after his death being taken to a secret location by his faithful band and placed in an unmarked grave, as the fear of his remains being targeted by an unforgiving establishment for revenge once they found its whereabouts was too great. Only a few trusty followers knew the place, and locked it in their hearts, leaving only a riddle as a clue for the faithful to come. Did his last arrow from his longbow really fly into the forest - or was it symbolic of his spirit taking flight? Was his body; bereft of spirit; laid to rest back from whence he came - in Sherwood Forest ?

I will follow the old straight track of the riddle and try to find out. I wonder............ will he still be there ?

The Quest continues; the Legend goes On........

Two ladies hunting a stag with a hound and bow and arrows in the medieval period

Appendix One

The English Longbow

The bow was a tool known since ancient times; a simple artifact found in a neolithic cave inhabited circa 10,000 years BC is thought to be a tool for straightening arrow shafts over a fire. The bow's power was in its simple construction, and its ability to put meat on the dining table. The Saxons and Danes had them, but disdained their use in battle as an impersonal weapon. In England around 1200, they were about five and a half feet long, made from yew or ash. They shot cloth-yard [*1] long arrows (30 to 36 inches long, made out of beech with a goose feather fletching) fitted with broad-bladed arrows that sliced into a quarry, causing instant death in the right spot or a slow leakage of blood from the wound that could be followed easily by the hunter until in range of a long knife for the coup de grace.

They were used in battles in the hands of skirmishers (individual archers advancing in front of the main battle line of armoured foot-soldiers) such as Hastings; King Harold of England is traditionally wounded by an arrow striking him in the eye [*2] from a hired archer from France before William's Normandy knights reached him and hacked him into pieces. After the use of them for the first time as part of an army by Edward I at the battle of Falkirk in 1298 (although details of their organisation by Edward escapes me, other than by word of mouth they turned up at an appointed spot, for pay) they had become fearsome and powerful weapons of war made from ash with a draw of around one hundred and fifty pounds, they were sending bodkin piles sharp-pointed armour-piercing arrows - from a solid line of disciplined men into both men and horses even when clad in armour an eighth of an inch thick at ranges up to 200 yards. Arrows would begin to rain down at a range of 350 yards on any unprotected billmen and horses causing pain, fear and ensuing panic. The archers would then join the rest of the infantry in making the most of the chaos.

At the battles of Crecy, Poitiers and Agincourt, it was the archers that won the day, although the English were heavily outnumbered by armoured knights of the French nobility. The common man had narrowed the gap; at Agincourt the flower of the French aristocracy was humbled as they fell off their dead or dying horses in the arrow storm from the mud-spattered, sick and hungry archers of Henry V standing in the English line. They and the rest of the infantry then ran into the disorganised ranks of the French armour and clubbed, stabbed and slashed into submission anyone left alive.

Kent, Welsh and Cheshire men had already established themselves as extraordinary bowmen before this; being encouraged by financial gain and statute to train regularly from an early age, they performed astounding feats of marksmanship and power [*3] which professional archers find difficulty in matching today (although some primitive archers come close!). The bows found on the resurrected wreck of Henry VIII's flagship Mary Rose are formidable weapons of great power, recreations of which defy drawing except by skilled archers today. The tremendous confidence this gave to ordinary common men unclad in armour gave them a terrific morale and esprit de corps, and made their services sought after by anyone raising an army.

It was a basic part of the English character later exploited by the Duke of Wellington that enabled men to stand in an outnumbered line and steadily deal out death to an enemy coming at them in circumstances which were generally successful against other European foes, who had often took to their heels at the first sight of an armoured mass on horseback coming at them.

The main opposition to the introduction of rifled firearms into military strategy at the end of the 18th century was that it enabled the common man to knock over his betters at long-range. Many British officers who suffered the loss of their friends at the hands of individual rifle-armed hunters during the American Revolution still did not want to see them used by their men; it reduced warfare to a science, and removed the luck factor. Although there was a lot of lead flying around on a Georgian battlefield, it was thought arbitrary bad luck to be struck by one, especially at ranges over a hundred yards. Accuracy made warfare less of a sport conducted by gentlemen, whose task on a battlefield was not to use a weapon but to direct their men as one, and set a good example whilst doing so. By giving the common soldier a weapon to enable him to literally have the power of life and death of an enemy officer in his hands it might very quickly be adopted by the enemy, and make British officers in return the hunted instead of the hunter.

The green-jacketed Riflemen of the Peninsula War 1808-1814 were seen to be the equivalent of the archers of Agincourt sitting on their damp ridge in 1415; helping to beat another army four hundred years later on a similarly wet ridge in 1815 at Waterloo [*4] which also vastly outnumbered them in prowess and size - in the same way as the khaki-clad soldiers of the British EF in their scrapes in 1914 carried on their traditions of accurate fire [*5]. In modern warfare, the flechette (arrow) has seen a return to the battlefield in the form of multiple pointed barbs propelled by explosives, slicing into a soldier and causing injuries making removal even by trained staff almost impossible.

The traditions of Robin Hood and the traditional English longbow are still very much alive today, in the loving care and safe hands of many hundreds of archers; many of whom dress traditionally [*6]. The Robin Hood Festival in Sherwood Forest [*7] attracts thousands of visitors each year who come to meet Robin Hood, the Merry Men, the Sheriff of Nottingham and his cronies, Richard The Lionheart and many others - including recently Herne the Hunter - in a colourful and light-hearted three-day spectacle. Excellent displays of archery and jousting, with minstrels and jesters, plays and story-tellers alongside make it a must for any Robin Hood enthusiast. A similar event, The Robin Hood Pageant, takes place later in the year at Nottingham Castle.

Footnotes
1. In the book The English Longbowman (excellently illustrated by Gerry Embleton) the author Clive Bartlett explains how this widely accepted historical description of the length of arrows is based on a misprint !

2. Since claimed to have been proved to be incorrect but in folklore generally held to be fact.

3. I was once shown an ancient castle door made of oak two inches thick several bodkin piles were still in it, protruding from the inner side, fired from longbows during a siege. Two feature films made of Shakespeare's Henry V give when viewed together an excellent visual representation of a medieval battle (including the arrow-storm) although of course with no detached body parts, and only the requisite amount of blood needed for the desired effect without upsetting the censor too much. I recommend watching them to give your imagination a leg-up (pardon the pun).

4. After the battle, the common flintlock infantry musket issued to the redcoats was shown to be so inferior to the longbow in battlefield performance that the Royal Toxophilite Society (patron, H.M. Prince Regent later King George IV) enjoyed a lot of support in suggesting that the traditional longbow replaced this firearm !

5. And they in turn were saved from encirclement by their enemies - in legend, anyway - by the old archers of Agincourt and the Angel of Mons

6. Many longbowmen wear traditional leather quivers and other accoutrements. In competition archery, there is a rule that only garments in the two colours green or white may be worn by the competing archers, reflecting the old lincoln green and linen of their ancestors.

7. Details of the festival and pageant and the current dates of the next ones can be obtained from the Nottinghamshire Tourist Office (tel 01623-822944)

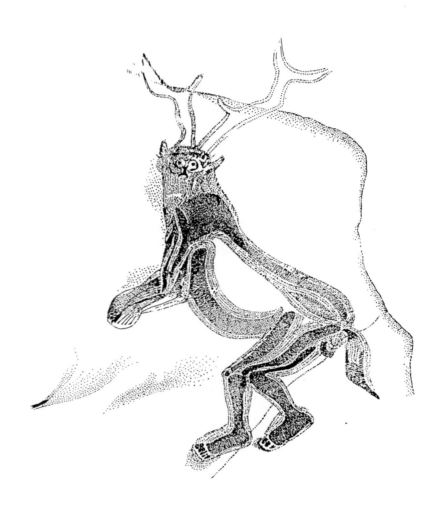

A stag-horned man dancing; from a 30,000 year old cave-painting

Appendix Two

Part One: The Oak and the Deer

No seeker of Robin Hood should omit a study of the folklore and ancient beliefs of our island. It is an integral part of the legend and its continuity particularly the rituals associated with sexual coupling at Beltane, which give us the surnames in perpetuity of Robs-son and Hobs-son, John's-son and Jacks-son conceived by Maid Marian but fathered by Robin Hood and Little John at Maytime revels (I try not to use the word orgy as it gives a wrong impression to modern minds) by men who were not quite themselves at the time !

The oak is well-known for its strength and durability. Both the Royal Navy and old London Bridge were built on its foundations. The Greeks and Romans saw the acorn as a fertility symbol in its resemblance to the *glans penis*; mistletoe when it grew upon it was highly regarded as its juice was said to be semen. In pre-Christian times, it was common for couples to be wed under an oak tree, and druids to worship their Goddess there. The oak itself symbolises long life; coffins were made from oak before its scarcity beginning in the 14th century perhaps to pass onto the future contents a vestige of their life?

Each year, the deer grow new antlers having shed the ones grown the year before. It is a continuous cycle. In 10,000BC a group of hunters settled at Star Carr near Scarborough, Yorkshire. They left (as were subsequently found in the excavations) many venerations of the deer, including a skull-cap made of antlers intended to be worn on the head, as shown in an ancient cave painting. Whole deer young pregnant does - were sunk in a nearby lake, their bellies filled with stones as a sacrifice to the gods for continuing fertility and a successful future hunt. The stag is sacred to the old goddess Diana, or Artemis; goddess of the Hunt. A burial in Wiltshire was filled with skeletons with their skulls deliberately bashed in, but had in their midst an antler; a token of rebirth and thanks from someone in the midst of the sacrifice?

At Abbots Bromley in Staffordshire, an ancient yearly ritual still survives. six dancers in the Horn Dance wear an antlered head-dress, coloured alternately black and white. They dance opposite to each other, then lock horns, and finally dance in a circle until another member - Robin Hood - shoots them with arrows. Maid Marian also participates in the dance, dipping a ladle in and out of a basin in time to the music, seen as representing the act of sexual coupling.

The ancient Chinese knew of the healing properties of antler, ground into a powder and taken for medicinal and rejuvenative purposes.

During the Middle Ages in England, the Green Man still figures prominently, sometimes named the Wodewose (from the Saxon meaning wild man of the woods). He dies every midsummer and is reborn in December, as a young child who grows with the earth in springtime. As a man, he sprouts antlers from his forehead and green growth issues from his mouth. This same belief has the Tree of Life an oak having three roots; one in the home of the Gods, one in the home of man on earth, and the other in the Underworld. The oak and the deer are bound up in this circle of death and rebirth.

How much more revered would a man be who in strict obedience to these two beliefs lived in close association with one, and slew the other in order to sustain and renew his life ?

Part Two:

Simple Survival

Not many of today's folk know what it is like to have to survive in the outdoors for a prolonged period. You are the hunted; a prey for many sorts of foe, in an environment that you neither know or understand and stand at a terrific disadvantage the forest is a living thing, an environment that has had thousands of years to establish itself. It goes on with its existence - and completely ignores you. You will have to fight for a place in it; fighting both It and Yourself. The first lesson that you are taught is psychological - Willpower you have to want to do it. Many who try fall at this first hurdle, simply lying down, giving up, and going into the sleep from which there is no awakening on this Earth.

You'll need tools; the only place you will find them is right in front of you. But where to look, and what for? Shelter is needed, to keep out of the worst of the weather. How to make fire? You'll eventually require new clothes, too.

A working knowledge of local flora and fauna is a great advantage; many will also die of starvation surrounded by nourishment, but be unable to recognise it. Some may be unable to deal with the still-warm body of an animal or cold clammy fish lying in front of them, or even figure out how to skin, joint, cook and eat it. Some will fall as a result of eating the wrong sort of food perhaps of poison, although this is rare - most will suffer first from sickness, exposure, disease and then give up through weakness and boredom. The microbe has killed far more men than any wild beast ever did.

The survivor, after a few weeks or months - perhaps years will have experienced - many times - the basic emotions of fear and hunger. They will have taken on and survived tremendous pressures; pared down from the original lost soul to one who now uses his knowledge as both provider, protector and weapon. They now have a pride, in themselves and their abilities. They also have confidence; no longer are they an intruder, but have fought for and gained a place in the scheme of things. They probably kill for meat, and harvest provender maybe even sow seeds. They still live from day to day, but now they have allies to rely on albeit hanging on a slender thread.

There is one simple ally that can be of enormous assistance. In the world of survival training, there is an old proverb Where One man can Survive, Two men can Fare Well. The ally that we most need is Companionship. Without a human friend, we could invent one (usually on the way to losing our sanity) and give it a name god, in the most extreme cases - giving it power and our worship in return for the company. Many men have died happy in loneliness with this god at their side. With human friends, you can build. You can talk, you can reason, and pass on skills and learning. You can draw on each others strengths and support each others weaknesses. A leader emerges in the pair or group; a little god perhaps, but in a visible form that you can talk to and touch. You are lucky to have your god with you each day in your trials, to touch and talk to. He will accept your worship gratefully as it gives him strength.

The outdoor way of life - although apparently idyllic as visualised in painting and poem, if you can hack it, left us thousands of years ago. We have forgotten too much, and can only now taste it between decent intervals. If you are a survivor by reason, outcast or fault - and most people are - the only way you will really survive, having surmounted all your environmental problems and earned a place in it and your self respect, is to take your destiny in your two hands and take the fight right back to the Enemy that put you there in the first place.

Appendix Three

A Brief Yearly Anthology of Robin Hood

1154	The first mention of Sherwood Forest by name
1266	Sheriff William de Grey waging war on the outlaws in Sherwood Forest
1304	Robin Hood named in the *Registrum Premonstratense*
1341	John Fordun (the Scots chronicler) names Robin Hood for the year 1266
1377	*Piers Plowman* first published, naming rhymes of Robin Hood
1420	Wynton names Robin Hood in the Scots Chronicles for the year 1283
1450	*Robin Hood and the Monk published*
1475	*Robin Hood and the Sheriff published*
1500	*Robin Hood and the Potter published*

1508-1594	*The Lyttle Geste of Robin Hood*; and many other ballads printed by Wynken de Worde
1598	Anthony Munday's play in which Robin becomes Earl of Huntingdon
1632	*The True Story of Robin Hood* published
1746	Stukeley publishes Robin Hood / Earl of Huntingdon's pedigree
1795	Ritson's *Life of Robin Hood*
1840	Pierce Egans story for children *Robin Hood & Little John*
1852	Hunter's examination of the legends published
1938	Warner Bros *Adventures of Robin Hood* starring Errol Flynn
1952	Walker's *True History of Robin Hood* published
1986	*The Quest for Robin Hood* written by Jim Lees

Appendix Four

On the Outlaw Trail at Home

Some suggested further reading :

The Quest for Robin Hood by Jim Lees; Temple Nostalgia Press, Nottingham (Excellent life study by Nottingham's Mr Robin Hood)

Robin Hood by Professor J C Holt; Thames & Hudson Press (A geographical and historical examination of the legend in detail)

Rymes of Robin Hood by R B Dobson & J Taylor; Alan Sutton Press
(Excellent compendium of the ballads and stories, with an introduction)

Robin Hood and the Lords of Wellow by Tony Molyneux-Smith; Nottinghamshire County Council Press
(An attributation of the legend to a Notts family and village)

Any local library will provide many of the other excellent books relating to the ballads of Robin Hood, early medieval life and the feudal system, knights and archery.

Some suggested films to watch :

The Adventures of Robin Hood (1938) Don't miss this one ! Errol Flynn; claimed to be the definitive portrayal of Robin Hood and from which most visualisations are still based today.

Henry V (1945) with Laurence Olivier; Henry V (1990) with Kenneth Branagh - atmospheric visuals, depicting medieval mentality and weaponry; and the ensuing carnage when employed.

Robin and Marian (1976) starring Sean Connery and Audrey Hepburn; with an excellent performance by Robert Shaw as the Sheriff of Nottingham.

Robin Of Sherwood (1984)- the television series. A series of compilation videos are available; the successful soundtrack by Clannad is also available on tape and compact disc.

Robin Hood; Prince of Thieves (1991), starring Kevin Costner; the only Robin Hood where the Sheriff steals the show!

Robin Hood; Men in Tights (1993) Nuff said - but light relief and a good laugh nevertheless. I think Robin Hood himself would have loved it!

Braveheart (1995), starring Mel Gibson. Again, recommended for historical atmosphere rather than adherence to historical fact; Patrick McGoohan gives an excellent interpretation of the aged King Edward I of England.

Some places and people to see in and around Nottingham in addition to those in the text :

The Tales of Robin Hood, Maid Marian Way, Nottingham (tel 0115 9483284)
100 metres from the Castle. An enjoyable trip through the forest and the legends via electric cablecar, ending with informative displays including have-a-go archery. Costumed guides, excellent refreshments area, good range of souvenirs and books to suit all pockets; overall very good value for money. Evening medieval banquets by arrangement; good victuals with wine or ale in pleasant atmospheric surroundings, with lovely serving wenches and characters from the legend to entertain you !

The Caves of Nottingham, Broad Marsh Shopping Centre, Nottingham
A Walkman-guided path through large caves and tunnels discovered when the shopping arcade was built, typical of those which still honeycomb most of the surrounding hill the city centre stands on. Good atmosphere; but it can be damp and a bit claustrophobic in places. Admission price is reasonable. With souvenir shop; the caves can get crowded on Bank Holidays and at odd times during school holidays.

You can see a few odd caves still in situ by walking through the Lace Market area or Castle Boulevard. Some served as simple dwellings, others as hermitages (as at Lenton) or holy sanctuaries. Some excellent small low-priced booklets on Nottingham's unique cave systems by local historians are available from Nottingham Library Shop.

Nottingham Castle
The Castle Museum & art gallery, Brewhouse Yard, Museum of Clothing and the Lace Museum are well worth a visit. Explanatory plaques around the castle site explain how the site evolved, and you can follow the plaques through

Nottingham on the City History Trails; or buy a ticket and take the brief trip by small bus from the Gatehouse. The castle is open for free in the week but an admission charge is made at weekends. A tearoom inside offers drinks and snacks, and there is a souvenir shop. The castle houses the Regimental Museum of the Worcester & Sherwood Foresters. Guided tours of the caves and tunnels in the castle rock are stunning; and more are being opened up all the time (available by arrangement courtesy of members of the Nottingham Civic Society) or check for the tour times on 0115 932 5769. Special historical events are held on the Castle Green throughout the year.

Allow at least four hours to see everything, including the cave trip.

Sherwood Forest Visitor Centre, Edwinstowe
(tel 01623 824490)
450 acres of ancient forest to walk through, featuring many ancient birch stands, beech and stag-headed oaks; the Robin Hood's Sherwood Forest exhibition, souvenirs, information centre and heritage trail, adventure playground and wildlife displays, maps and route guides. Places everywhere for picnics, but a spacious tea room at the centre also offers the usual refreshments for both young and old. Free admission; although a small charge is made sometimes for car parking and the exhibition theatre depending on any special events such as period archery which are held throughout the year. The versatile Forest Rangers take out forest treks to show special areas of the forest including the local flora and fauna to tourists and school parties (which are very popular, and should be pre-booked to prevent any disappointment). Details of these are published in a yearly booklet. Watch out for the outlaws if you visit here during the school holidays - one of them might be me!

The World of Robin Hood, Haughton near Retford
(tel 01623 860210)
A recreated medieval village, with parts of the film sets from the film *Robin Hood; Prince of Thieves*. Reconstructed and manned by costumed guides, talking you through the time tunnels into the everyday life of the medieval peasant, nobleman and the Crusades circa AD1190. Special events are held here on Bank Holidays including falconry (phone for details). The site is now mostly under cover; large reasonably priced restaurant and bar.

The Wolfshead Bowmen
A historical re-enactment and living history group who travel to historic sites and castles throughout England, giving period displays of the daily life, food, longbow, arms and armour of the medieval man and woman. Anyone wishing to live the part after reading this guide can apply for membership; at the Robin Hood Festival each year this group camp at the Major Oak and become Robin Hood and his Merry Men! For membership details, access their website or the author.

Nottinghamshire Tourist Office
Rufford Abbey, Ollerton
(tel 01623 822944)
Information on future events and help with general inquiries including accommodation.

MIDAS HISTORIC TOURS
Tel 01932-831155
Offering varied and exciting tours to many UK and foreign locations, with guides who are picked for their knowledge and affability. The author as *Rifleman Moore* currently guides Sharpe's Peninsula (Wellington's campaigns in Portugal and Spain 1808-1814), Waterloo 1815 (Napoleon's Final Defeat) and The Crimean War around Sevastopol. Plans are afoot for another tour for 1999 - *The Legend of Robin Hood*!

Epílogue

*Three times in my life I have been present when a life hung by
a thread*

Your past schooling, training and character whirl about you
as in a kaleidoscope and suddenly focus on the sight in front
of you; all else is in darkness. If - at that moment - it is your
hand on the scalpel; your hands on the firehose; your
authority in a violent situation; your pen poised over the
proposed cuts in a budget; or your finger on the trigger - you
have a difficult decision to make.

To take from the "rich" - or Give to the "poor".........

When you sacrifice a bit of yourself for others, lend a hand,
make a stand for your rights, strike a blow for freedom, say a
word for the underdog - or simply Forgive someone - you add
to the "rich" quality of Life. There are many men and women
out there in the everyday world who do this on a daily basis,
sacrificing a bit of themselves for the good of all. You may
have met some of them already; some you are yet to meet -
but they are always there when you need them. They look
after us, watch over us, rescue us, nurse us and care for us.
Without them, we'd be lost.

If you turn your back on all this and indulge in simple avarice
and greed at the expense of your fellow man you might end up
walking about with a pocketful of money, but you'll be quite
alone .. and really quite "poor".

Do as our ancient ancestors did; look up into the night sky, thirteen times a year after the darkness. Ancient legends of Greece and Rome placed their Heroes in the starry constellations; so look up and find the largest and brightest light. You will see Robin Hood's bow standing there above you, bent and ready to shoot -- sometimes you'll see the arrows from it streaking through the night. You can see Him in the daytime too - if you look - reflected in the eyes, hearts and actions of thousands of everyday heroes that you pass in the street without a second glance.

I hope this inspires the reader, as it has always inspired me.

Three times in my life I have seen Robin Hood!

Conclusion

If you shuffle through the stories like a pack of playing cards and put them in a sort of 'non-chronological order', add some later tales and also some parts of others - there is a kind of surprising continuity in it all! There is a thread you can follow through all the stories ; the central themes also link them together. Many story, script and screenplay writers have also spotted this 'sense from non-sense' aspect and spun some extremely clever tales by doing so [*5].

One example I use is to add a more modern story to Robin and the King and put Robin and Maid Marian before it; insert Maid Marian's death into the beginning of *The Death of Robin Hood* and have her buried in the chapel that Robin goes off to visit in the 'Geste' after leaving the Kings' court, and then spends twenty-two years as a solitary hermit there faithful to her memory still accompanied by the faithful Little John, before finally coming out of this voluntary solitary confinement through old age and dying when betrayed. Little John can then take Robin's body off to a secret location - contained in a local folk-riddle - back to the chapel where Friar Tuck resides to be buried and lie side by side with Marian forever. John goes away on a 'pilgrimage' to forget the loss of his friend, returning home years later to live out his life at Hathersage.

Including Marian's death is complex; a 'touchy' subject for storytellers as it changes Robin's personality completely (suggesting almost semi-insanity) and re-introduces the murder or 'revenge' theme. It can explain Robin's devotions, why he left the King, and why the previously missing prophecy of the wise-woman tells he will finally die for - not by - a 'woman's hand'. I put all this together one day to amuse myself and my friends; it does tie up all the loose ends and make a complete, romantic and adventurous tale whenever read.

There are obvious comparisons to the tales of King Arthur and other 'heroes'. One can speculate endlessly on these aspects of the stories; the stories themselves have been shown many times already to be able to mean and say anything anyone wishes. This flexibility to change like a chameleon to suit almost any background, and the continuing debates over the 'real' Robin Hood's birth, life and death that has ensued has so far lasted almost as long as the legend of Robin Hood itself. I leave the present readers to join the rest of us sitting around this theoretical campfire and having once warmed themselves, contribute to the debate if they wish [*6].

Footnotes

1. All dealing mostly with places up and down the old medieval main roads to York between there and Nottingham, passing through the two main wooded areas of Barnsdale and, of course, Sherwood.

2. There are as many storybooks in all shapes and sizes as there are tales; they are far too numerous to list here. Some of the 'antique' ones I have in my collection here are complete with marvellous illustrations in colour - and I'm still finding new ones to add to them each year.

3. When the author suggested that a derivative of a 'natural poison' such as belladonna, digitalis or aconitum disguised and administered in a strong cordial would be the best way of 'doing away' with a trusting semi-invalid under these circum-

stances, he referred it to a detective specialising in homicide who has always offered sound advice on this grisly subject. What he said in reply was - as ever - sound, logical and altogether reasonable (see footnote 4 below).

4. There is a continuing mailbag to a fictional character which began well before the turn of the century. The postman still delivers a weekly mailbag with letters addressed to 'Mr Sherlock Holmes, 221b Baker Street, London'. When the author wrote conceming Robin's death in connection with this book - he did receive a reply.

5. Most notably recently in the highly successful television series 'Robin of Sherwood'.

6. Or even try to ask Robin Hood himself; the 'Grimston Ghost' is said to be Robin Hood and appears at intervals complete with hood and carrying his longbow near s Nottinghamshire village in Sherwood Forest. So far the author has not managed in three previous attempts managed to make contact with him - but that won't stop hin trying again in the future !

A selection of other Capall Bann titles. Free catalogue available.

Dragons of the West by Nigel Pennick

For thousands of years fabulous serpents and dragons have been the stuff of myth and traveller's tales. The dragon has held the attention of people for centuries, and continues to do so. The dragon is more than a beast of tall stories, myth and folk-tale, for it is a symbol of the awesome power of nature which appears in many variant forms, but which we can understand only in symbolic or allegorical form. Thus, it appears in religious symbolism, alchemy, medicine and geomancy as well as in the more lyrical tales of bards and storytellers. Ultimately the dragon is a product of the human mind, for there are dragons of various kinds lurking deep within us all. This book explores Western dragon and dragonslayer traditions, not just legends, but living festivals and rituals surviving today. ISBN 1 86163 007 7   £10.95

Handbook of Fairies by Ronan Coghlan

Many theories have been put forward about fairies - whether their origins are the deities of pre-Christian religions, primitive peoples driven into hiding, or even the denizens of UFOs.This is a detailed guide to fairies and other otherworldly beings. The different types of fairy and other otherworld beings are described, together with stories and legends about them. The possible origins of fairies are also discussed as are various theories about them, their links or differences from aliens, the passing of time in the Otherworld and other fascinating topics. Beautiful illustrations. ISBN 186163 042 5   £9.95

The Magical History of the Horse by Janet Farrar and Virginia Russell

This book traces the magical history of the horse throughout the centuries and explores its connections with paganism, mythology, Biblical and Christian lore, folklore and fairytale, healing and superstition. Loved, feared or venerated, the horse has become integrated with human work, warfare, history and sport. It has become the living symbol of many gods and goddesses, the prototype of many mythical beasts. Janet Farrar, established writer on magic and mythology and Virginia Russell, a lifelong horsewoman, combine their talents in this exploration of the horse's magical history. A veritable harvest of the legends, magical concepts and folk beliefs that have surrounded the horse from the dawn of history to the present day. ISBN 186163 033 6   £10.95

A Romany Tapestry by Michael Hoadley

Always interested in alternative lifestyles and alternative medicine, Michael Hoadley started collecting Romany lore and remedies. This book is the result of a lifetime's association with Romany Gypsies, much of it written from a personal point of view. This is a comfortable, fireside book with something to interest everyone - Romany origins, practices, beliefs customs and lore, healing remedies and tales. An intensely personal book about a little-known people who live life to the full in their own very individual ways. ISBN 186163 067 0   £7.95

Arthur - The Legend Unveiled by Christopher Johnson and Eve Lung

This fascinating book explores the Arthurian legends from a Pagan rather than the later Christian perspective. Divinity, in the original Celtic religion, was viewed as the Goddess and the Queen as her representative, held the sovereignty of the land. Arthur is first favoured by the Goddess, but ambition leads him to turn to Christianity, belittling Gwenivere's power and avoiding participation in challenges to his Kingship by younger, vital men. This, rather than the Christianised, "moral failings" of individuals, is what leads to the Wasteland and Arthur's eventual downfall. This book presents a fresh and challenging view of the Arthurian Legend. ISBN 1898307 61X   £9.95

FREE DETAILED CATALOGUE

A detailed illustrated catalogue is available on request, SAE or International Postal Coupon appreciated. **Titles can be ordered direct from Capall Bann, post free in the UK** (cheque or PO with order) or from good bookshops and specialist outlets. Titles currently available include:

Angels and Goddesses - Celtic Christianity & Paganism by Michael Howard
Arthur - The Legend Unveiled by C Johnson & E Lung
Auguries and Omens - The Magical Lore of Birds by Yvonne Aburrow
Caer Sidhe - Celtic Astrology and Astronomy by Michael Bayley
Call of the Horned Piper by Nigel Jackson
Celtic Lore & Druidic Ritual by Rhiannon Ryall
Crossing the Borderlines - Guising, Masking & Ritual Animal Disguise in the
  European Tradition, Nigel Pennick
Earth Dance - A Year of Pagan Rituals by Jan Brodie
Earth Magic by Margaret McArthur
Enchanted Forest - The Magical Lore of Trees by Yvonne Aburrow
Familiars - Animal Powers of Britain by Anna Franklin
Healing Homes by Jennifer Dent
Herbcraft - Shamanic & Ritual Use of Herbs by Sue Lavender & Anna Franklin
In Search of Herne the Hunter by Eric Fitch
Magical Guardians - Exploring the Spirit & Nature of Trees by Philip Heselton
Magical Lore of Cats by Marion Davies
Magical Lore of Herbs by Marion Davies
Masks of Misrule - The Horned God & His Cult in Europe by Nigel Jackson
Sacred Animals by Gordon MacLellan
Sacred Grove - The Mysteries of the Forest by Yvonne Aburrow
Sacred Geometry by Nigel Pennick
Sacred Lore of Horses The by Marion Davies
Sacred Ring - Pagan Origins British Folk Festivals & Customs by Mike Howard
Seasonal Magic - Diary of a Village Witch by Paddy Slade
Secret Places of the Goddess by Philip Heselton

Our list is expanding rapidly so do contact us for details on the latest releases.

Capall Bann Publishing, Freshfields, Chieveley, Berks, RG20 8TF